The Approved Mental Health Professional's Guide to Psychiatry and Medication

Post-qualifying Social Work Practice – titles in the series

Adult Social Work in Practice .... ISBN 978 1 84445 292 7

The Approved Mental Health Professional's
Guide to Mental Health Law (2nd ed) .... ISBN 978 1 84445 062 6

The Approved Mental Health Professional's Guide to
Psychiatry and Medication (2nd ed) .... ISBN 978 1 84445 304 7

Critical Thinking for Social Work (2nd ed) .... ISBN 978 1 84445 049 7

Evidence-Based Policy and Practice in Mental Heath
Social Work .... ISBN 978 1 84445 149 4

The Integration of Mental Health Social Work and the NHS   ISBN 978 1 84445 150 0

Introducing Child Care Social Work .... ISBN 978 1 84445 180 7

Law and the Social Work Practitioner (2nd ed) ...... ISBN 978 1 84445 264 4

Leadership, Management and Supervision in Health
and Social Care .... ISBN 978 1 84445 181 4

Managing with Plans and Budgets in Health and Social Care   ISBN 978 1 84445 134 0

The Mental Capacity Act 2005: A Guide for Practice (2nd Ed)   ISBN 978 1 84445 129 6

Practising Quality Assurance in Social Care .... ISBN 978 1 84445 084 8

Social Work Practice with Older Lesbians and Gay Men   ISBN 978 1 84445 182 1

To order, please contact our distributor: BEBC Distribution, Albion Close, Parkstone, Poole, BH12 3LL. Telephone: 0845 230 9000, email:learningmatters@bebc.co.uk. You can also find more information on each of these titles and our other learning resources at www.learningmatters.co.uk.

The Approved Mental Health Professional's Guide to Psychiatry and Medication

Second Edition

ROBERT BROWN

GWEN ADSHEAD

ALAN POLLARD

Series Editor: Keith Brown

LearningMatters

First published in 2007 by Learning Matters Ltd
This edition published 2009

British Library Cataloguing in Publication Data
A CIP record for this book is available from the British Library

ISBN: 978 1 84445 304 7

Cover and text design by Code 5 Design Associates Ltd
Project Management by Deer Park Productions, Tavistock, Devon
Typeset by Pantek Arts Ltd, Maidstone, Kent
Printed and bound in Great Britain by Bell & Bain Ltd, Glasgow

Learning Matters Ltd
33 Southernhay East
Exeter EX1 1 NX
Tel: 01392 215560
info@learningmatters.co.uk
www.learningmatters.co.uk

Mixed Sources
Product group from well-managed
forests and other controlled sources
www.fsc.org Cert no. TT-COC-002769
© 1996 Forest Stewardship Council
FSC

Contents

List of abbreviations   vii

About the authors   ix

Foreword from the series editor   xi

Preface   xiii

1   The importance of psychiatry and medication for

    Approved Mental Health Professionals   1

2   Psychiatrists: training and how they practise   5

3   An overview of psychiatry and classificiation   12

4   Psychotic disorders   16

5   Neurotic disorders, substance abuse and
    personality disorders   21

6   Forensic psychiatry   32

7   Psychiatry of old age   40

8   Psychiatry and risk assessment   45

9   Patients as parents   50

10 Child and adolescent psychiatry   61

11 Treatment issues in psychiatry 67

12 Classification of medication in psychiatry 71

13 Anti-depressants and mood stabilisers 74

14 Anti-psychotics (*BNF* section 4.2) 82

15 Anxiolytics and sedative/hypnotics (*BNF* section 4.1) 88

16 Older adults, children, unlicensed drugs 94

17 The law and psychiatric treatment 100

18 Treatment under the Mental Health Act 108

Statutes 117

Case law 117

Some useful websites 119

References 121

Index 123

List of abbreviations

AC	approved clinician
ADD	attention deficit disorder
ADHD	attention deficit hyperactivity disorder
AMHP	Approved Mental Health Professional
ASPD	anti-social personality disorder
BAN	British Approved Name
BNF	British National Formulary
BPD	borderline personality disorder
BPSD	behavioural and psychological symptoms of dementia
CBT	cognitive-behavioural therapy
CCW	Care Council for Wales
CHEI	cholinesterase inhibitor
CMHT	community mental health team
CPCC	child protection case conference
CQC	Care Quality Commission
CSM	Committee on the Safety of Medicines
DSH	deliberate self-harm
DSM	Diagnostic and Statistical Manual
ECT	electro-convulsive therapy
EMS	eosinophilia myalgia syndrome
EPS	extrapyramidal symptoms
GSCC	General Social Care Council
HIV	human immunosuppressive virus
HIW	Healthcare Inspectorate Wales
ICD	International Classification of Diseases
IMCA	Independent Mental Capacity Advocate
IMHA	Independent Mental Health Advocate
LPA	lasting power of attorney

LSSA	Local Social Services Authority
MAD	major affective disorder
MAOI	monoamine-oxidase inhibitor
MCMHP	Member of the College of Mental Health Pharmacists
MHRA	Medicines and Healthcare Products Regulatory Agency
MHRT	Mental Health Review Tribunal
MHT	Mental Health Tribunal (for Wales)
MMSE	Mini Mental State Examination
MSE	mental state examination
NARI	noradrenaline re-uptake inhibitor
NaSSA	noradrenergic and specific serotonergic anti-depressant
NICE	National Institute for Health and Clinical Excellence
NPD	narcissistic personality disorder
NTIS	National Teratology Information Service
NRT	nicotine replacement therapy
OCD	obsessive–compulsive disorder
OPTICS	Optimax Information and Clinical Support
OTC	over the counter
PRN	'when necessary' (Latin: pro re nata)
PTSD	post-traumatic stress disorder
RC	Responsible Clinician
RIMA	reversible inhibitor of monoamine oxidase A
rINN	recommended International Non-proprietary Name
RMO	responsible medical officer
SCT	Supervised Community Treatment
SNRI	selective serotonin and norepinephrine re-uptake inhibitors
SOAD	second opinion appointed doctor
SPC	summary of product characteristics
SSRI	selective serotonin re-uptake inhibitor
TCA	tricyclic anti-depressant
TD	tardive dyskinesia

About the Authors

Rob Brown is Director of the Bournemouth University Approved Mental Health Professionals course in South West England. He is also a Mental Health Act Commissioner covering Dorset, and has been a member of the Commission since 1992. Rob previously worked as a Mental Welfare Officer and then as an Approved Social Worker with Hampshire County Council. He has been a lecturer at Southampton University, Stirling University and Croydon College. He contributes to the training of section 12 approved doctors and Approved Clinicians in South West England and Wales. Rob has published widely in the field of mental health and mental capacity law.

Gwen Adshead is a Consultant Psychiatrist and Psychotherapist for West London Mental Health NHS Trust based at Broadmoor High Secure Hospital. Dr Adshead has specialised in forensic psychiatry, mental health law and trauma psychiatry since 1987. In addition to being a practising clinician, she is also the author of several papers and book chapters, regularly teaches students and lectures at professional conferences. She is the co-editor of two journals.

Alan Pollard is Chief Pharmacist at the Worcestershire Mental Health Partnership NHS Trust. He has taught on ASW (now AMHP) courses for several years. Alan was the secretary of the United Kingdom Psychiatric Pharmacy Group from 1999 to 2001. He has written a number of papers as well as local protocols. He is currently involved with POMH-UK, the Prescribing Observatory for Mental Health, a national initiative designed to improve prescribing practice in specialist mental health services and to help local services to implement and monitor NICE guidance.

Foreword from the Series Editor

All texts in the Post-Qualifying Social Work Series have been written by people with a passion for excellence in social work practice. They are primarily written for social workers who are undertaking Post-Qualifying Social Work Awards; however they are clearly of value to any social worker who wants to consider up-to-date social work practice issues.

They are also of value to social work students as they are written to inform, inspire and develop social work practice. All the authors have a connection with the Centre for Post Qualifying Social Work. Rob Brown is Course Director for the AMHP course in South West England and used to have that role on the South London course. Gwen Adshead (psychiatrist) and Alan Pollard (pharmacist) contributed as lecturers on our AMHP courses for several years. This has enabled them to focus on issues of psychiatry and medication that are of particular relevance and interest to Approved Mental Health Professionals.

This text will be of interest to all professionals working in the field of mental health, not just AMHPs, and what is of great value is the practical nature of the text – it really will help you reflect on and consider your practice.

As a centre we are all committed to raising the profile of the social work profession. We trust that you will find this text of real value to your social work practice, and that this in turn will have a real impact on the service that users and carers receive.

Keith Brown
Series Editor
Centre for Post Qualifying Social Work
Bournemouth University

Preface

Welcome to the second edition of the *Approved Mental Health Professional's Guide to Psychiatry and Medication*. This has been designed primarily for those on an Approved Mental Health Professional course but it should also be useful for practising AMHPs, other mental health professionals, service users, carers and others interested in the field of mental health. There are some references to law with regard to consent to treatment. The legal examples given in the text relate to England and Wales. Note that the law is significantly different in Scotland, Northern Ireland, the Isle of Man and the Channel Islands.

There are some references to relevant competences which are now set out in Regulations (which differ slightly between England and Wales).

The law is changing rapidly in the mental health field. The guide is up to date as at April 2009. Readers may wish to check that there has been no major recent case law which alters the position as stated here. A good source website for this purpose can be found at **www.imhap.org.uk**.

Recent changes which are covered in this book include the impact of the Mental Health Act 2007. This affected the Mental Health Act 1983 with such changes as:

- a new definition of mental disorder;

- revised consent to treatment rules;

- the introduction of the Community Treatment Order;

- ASWs being replaced by AMHPs with a broader range of professionals;

- Responsible Medical Officers (RMOs) being replaced by Responsible Clinicians

  (RCs), again with a broader range of professionals able to take on the function.

The same 2007 Act amended the Mental Capacity Act 2005 by introducing Deprivation of Liberty Safeguards in response to the Bournewood case.

Finally the revised text also takes account of recent:

- case law on human rights challenges to the imposition of treatment;

- incapacity cases determined by the Courts where treatment was an issue.

There are two companion texts in this series. *The Approved Mental Health Professional's Guide to Mental Health Law* is issued to many trainee AMHPs. *The Mental Capacity Act 2005: A Guide for Mental Health Professionals* will also be useful to many readers. This contains a full copy of the text of the Mental Capacity Act. Those seeking a copy of the text of the Mental Health Act 1983 as revised may wish to see *Mental Health Law in England and Wales,* which is also published by Learning Matters.

There is significant overlap between mental health and mental capacity law. This book contains a brief summary of current law in both areas in so far as they affect treatment issues.

Chapters 12 to 15 link types of medication to the *British National Formulary* (*BNF*) system of classifying drugs. This should be useful, either in cases where you are making reference to consent to treatment forms (note that BNF classes are often used in Mental Health Act forms to indicate how many drugs in any class may be given) or in the event of your needing to look up further details in *BNF* itself. At the time of going to print the current *BNF* is Volume 57 dated March 2009. This is available from bookshops or on line at: **www.bnf.org/bnf** Please note that while principal brand names for drugs are given in brackets, many agents are available in generic form or as other brands. Please consult the latest *BNF* for further clarification. Drug names now reflect the new rINN (recommended International Non-proprietary Name) which supersedes the former BAN (British Approved Name). Where the two differ, the former BAN is given in lower case in adjacent parentheses (ban).

We are especially grateful to Rob Ferris, Isabel Paz and Virginia Valle Atela, who have all contributed material to this text, and to Ron Lacey who co-wrote our earlier guides.

Robert Brown, South West AMHP Programme Director,
c/o Institute of Health & Community Studies, Post Qualifying Social Work Team, Bournemouth University, 4th Floor, Royal London House, Christchurch Road, Bournemouth, BH1 3LT.

Chapter 1

The importance of psychiatry and medication for Approved Mental Health Professionals

The use of complusion

It may seem obvious that Approved Mental Health Professionals should have a good understanding of psychiatry and the use of medication in the treatment of mental disorders. After all, the very essence of the AMHP role is to determine whether compulsory treatment and care can be justified. It is a strange role requiring a mental health worker to take on a quasi-judicial function for a very specific decision concerning an individual. In the von Brandenburg case Lord Bingham identified the central role of the AMHP (then ASW) in this process. Although doctors make the recommendations it is the AMHP who makes the application (apart from those very rare case where the applicant is the nearest relative). To exercise this role effectively and fairly, AMHPs need to have a clear understanding of what will happen to a patient in terms of treatment within a psychiatric hospital if the AMHP decides to make the application. Equally they need to know what alternative treatments can realistically be given outside of the hospital. In November 2008 the Community Treatment Order was introduced requiring an AMHP's agreement to the order and its conditions before it can be implemented.

Treatment of mental illness

Medication is central to the treatment of mental illness in the UK. While other forms of mental disorder (such as learning disability and personality disorders) rely more on care and psychotherapeutic interventions, a very high proportion of mentally ill patients are treated with psychotropic drugs, so much so that debates about treatment and the use of compulsion often neglect other methods of intervention.

The Mental Health Act 1983 covers people who have a mental disorder, now defined broadly in section 1 of the Act as *any disorder or disability of the mind.* For long-term detention and for guardianship, patients with a learning disability have to pass a further test as to whether they exhibit abnormally aggressive or seriously irresponsible conduct.

Use of psychiatric labels in mental health law

The most obvious recent example of this issue is to be found in the debate leading up to the Mental Health Act 2007, which revised the 1983 Act. The changes were designed, among other things, to bring in a broad definition of mental disorder. One of the more controversial changes was to remove several of the previous exclusions, i.e. behaviours which by themselves could not be seen as a mental disorder (as per section 1 of the Mental Health Act 1983). The exclusion of sexual deviancy was seen as a problem by the government, which has changed this situation. Para 24 of the Explanatory Notes to the Mental Health Act states:

> there are disorders of sexual preference which are recognised clinically as mental disorders. Some of these disorders might be considered 'sexual deviance' in the terms of the current exclusion (for example paraphilias like fetishism or paedophilia). On that basis, the amendment would bring such disorders within the scope of the 1983 Act.

The government argument relied heavily on the fact that these paraphilias are included in ICD10. Classification is discussed in Chapter 3 of this book. There is also a critique of psychiatrists' approaches to classification.

Nearest relatives

When liaising with nearest relatives it is helpful if AMHPs have a working knowledge of treatment models and can point the relative to sources of further advice on any concerns they may have. A nearest relative's objection to admission on section 3 may relate to concerns over the proposed treatments.

SOAD consultations

Under Parts 4 and 4A of the Mental Health Act 1983 there are a number of occasions when Second Opinion Appointed Doctors (SOADs) have to consult someone who is not a doctor (and for Part 4 not a nurse). A significant number of these consultations involve Approved Mental Health Professionals because they have been professionally concerned with the patient. A knowledge of treatments and their likely benefits and problems is invaluable in this situation. After consultation the AMHP is now expected to record their involvement in the patient's medical record.

AMHP competences: the Regulations

In this volume we look at the relevant competences for England as set out in the Mental Health (Approved Mental Health Professionals) (Approval) (England) Regulations 2008. It should be noted that the Welsh equivalent is almost identical for the focus of this book. Regulation 3 states:

> *(1) An LSSA may only approve a person to act as an AMHP if it is satisfied that the person has appropriate competence in dealing with persons who are suffering from mental disorder.*
>
> *(2) In determining whether it is satisfied a person has appropriate competence, the LSSA must take into account the following factors:*
>
>> *(a) that the person fulfils at least one of the professional requirements; and*
>>
>> *(b) the matters set out in Schedule 2.*
>
> *(3) Before an LSSA may approve a person to act as an AMHP who has not been approved, or been treated as approved, before in England and Wales, the person must have completed within the last five years a course approved by the General Social Care Council or the Care Council for Wales.*

The most relevant competences which are covered in this book are:

3. Key Competence Area 3: Application of knowledge: Mental disorder

> *Whether the applicant has a critical understanding of, and is able to apply in practice:*
>
>> *(a) a range of models of mental disorder, including the contribution of social, physical and development factors;*
>>
>> *(b) the social perspective on mental disorder and mental health needs, in working with patients, their relatives, carers and other professionals;*
>>
>> *(c) the implications of mental disorder for patients, their relatives and carers; and*
>>
>> *(d) the implications of a range of treatments and interventions for patients, their relatives and carers.*

3(a) and (b) are particularly addressed in Chapters 2 to 11 where an overview of psychiatry as practised in the UK is given.

For competence 3(c) the effects of mental disorder are considered in many of the chapters. The last two chapters also provide useful information on the law relating to treatment, either under the Mental Health Act 1983, under the Mental Capacity Act 2005, or very occasionally under common law.

For competence 3(d) Chapters 11 to 16 provide detailed information on treatment for mental disorder with a detailed critique of the use of medication as part of psychiatric treatment.

Legal duty of the AMHP

Finally, in exercising their responsibilities under section 13(1A) of the Mental Health Act 1983 it will be recalled that where an AMHP is:

(a) *satisfied that such an application ought to be made in respect of the patient; and*

(b) *of the opinion, having regard to any wishes expressed by relatives of the patient or any other relevant circumstances, that it is necessary or proper for the application to be made by him,*

he shall make the application.

Subsection (2) then requires that

before making an application for the admission of a patient to hospital an approved mental health professional shall interview the patient in a suitable manner and satisfy himself that detention in a hospital is in all the circumstances of the case the most appropriate way of providing the care and medical treatment of which the patient stands in need.

This will include a consideration of the past history of the patient's mental disorder, the patient's present condition, the effect on this of any social, family and personal factors, the wishes of the patient, and medical opinion.

Although it is important to stress that the AMHP is acting on behalf of the local authority which is accountable for the AMHP's actions, it should be noted that the AMHP also carries a personal responsibility in making this decision.

A clear understanding of psychiatry and related treatment is essential to perform this role competently.

Chapter 2
Psychiatrists: training and how they practise

The medical model

Psychiatry is a branch of medicine and as such has been accounted as a natural science. This has been problematic for both medicine and psychiatry, because there are many aspects of health care which do not resemble traditional scientific activity at all. In particular, the traditional scientific approach to problem-solving tends to emphasise objective observation and data collection. In contrast, the subjective experience of patients is a crucial factor in both general medicine and psychiatry.

Psychiatrists have tended to adopt what is known as the 'medical model' when thinking about psychiatric illnesses and patients. There are in fact several versions of the 'medical model', but essentially what this implies is a pre-existing state which is defined as 'normal' which can then be rendered 'abnormal' by internal or external causes. Evidence of abnormality can be found in 'symptoms' of illness (what the patient complains of) or 'signs' of illness, which are generally only detectable by others, usually experts. The doctor's job is to recognise both the 'signs' and the 'symptoms', which then usually indicate what the underlying problem is.

EXAMPLE

A man complains of shortness of breath and a cough. The doctor notes these as symptoms, and then examines him for signs of chest disease. By examining his chest, he finds a sign (wheezes on inspiration). He notes another sign: that the man is coughing up green sputum. He therefore deduces that the man has a chest infection and prescribes antibiotics.

An essential feature of the medical model is that the underlying disease is treated rather than symptoms. In fact symptomatic relief alone is frowned on unless no other intervention is possible (or unless that symptom is pain). Another feature is that the patient's subjective account is generally of less importance than the signs that are detected on examination or after investigation, although the model also assumes that the patient's history is true and honestly given.

These features of the medical model cause problems for psychiatrists, and their patients. First, the psychiatrist has no means to investigate the brain or mind, such as X-rays or blood tests. Although some diseases that can be detected this way do cause psychiatric symptoms, they are not very common, and most of psychiatric practice relies only on the patient's subjective account. Second, the patient's own account may be hard to follow or interpret; it may indeed be the only 'sign' of illness that there is. The psychiatrist is therefore handicapped because their main informant may be unreliable. Lastly, given that the patient may not be able to tell others what is going on, the psychiatrist may have to rely on either information from others or on signs of mental illness manifested in behaviour. But behaviour is capable of many interpretations, and other people's accounts of the patient may say more about them than about the patient. Signs like a persistent cough or an abnormally raised level of some chemical in the blood usually only mean one thing; someone rocking back and forth may be communicating many things.

The medical model therefore may have some validity in general psychiatry but its use is limited by:

- a lack of knowledge about what constitutes 'normal' psychological functioning generally;
- a lack of knowledge about 'normal' neurological functioning and its relationship to psychological functioning;
- a lack of knowledge about what is 'normal' for this patient as an individual;
- the fact that there may be important elements of the patient's condition, which are not only to do with the patient as an individual but to do with his or her interaction with the environment and other persons.

Another difficulty with the medical model lies in psychiatry's continuing struggle for scientific respectability. Having to rely on the patient's account, and the lack of ways to corroborate or amplify this account objectively, means that psychiatry can be seen as hopelessly subjective. Worse still, there are psychiatrists who take this subjectivity seriously, and even suggest that their own subjective response to the patient may be informative. This intersubjective approach to human understanding may appear highly unscientific to those trained to approach medicine as a purely objective practice and therefore psychiatry remains a 'Cinderella' speciality among doctors. It is common for the lay public to be surprised when they hear that psychiatrists are medically qualified.

Lastly, the medical model assumes that the practice of medicine is a good thing, and that those who practise it are doing good. However, psychiatrists often find that they are not seen as 'good' by their patients at all, but instead may be seen as the enemy. They may have to take actions that the patient sees as both harmful and wrong; they may have to take sides against the patient. Not only are they not always popular with their patients, but also they are subject to the same public stigma as their patients. Doctors tend to be identified with the branch of medicine they practise, and it is a commonplace joke that all psychiatrists are 'mad' in a culture where mental illness is highly stigmatised.

There are some benefits from the use of the medical model in psychiatry. A medical approach to mental illness resulted in the use of anti-psychotic medication. The psychiatrists practising then (many of whom are now close to retirement) had a real experience of seeing people improve. Life in the hospitals before anti-psychotic medication was pretty grim, and psychiatrists working there saw something like a miracle, which profoundly affected them. Second, the miracle cure was really a 'medical' one: medication in dosages to be worked out by an expert, not just listening to people talking. Psychiatrists could be 'real' doctors doing 'real' good. Both these aspects pushed a generation of psychiatrists firmly into use of the medical model which has led to the development of services and the proper allocation of resources. By making mental distress an illness, there has been some increase in tolerance and decrease in stigma, so that mental illness can be talked about publicly and seen as a condition which can be treated.

What the medical model has resulted in is a reluctance by doctors to think about the differences between them and their patients: the sociology of psychiatry. Psychiatrists are often highly defensive about these differences, many of which apply to medicine as a whole. In the NHS, most psychiatrists come from middle-class, highly educated backgrounds; most patients will come from disadvantaged backgrounds. This is true, irrespective of ethnicity or culture. Money, class and education play an enormous role in mental illness; most mental illnesses are more common in working-class populations where there is more stress, usually as a result of unemployment, poor housing and poverty. Most outpatients are female, but most inpatients are male, and there is substantial over-representation of African-Caribbean and African patients in inpatient services. It is hard not to think that the differences between the assessing doctors and the patients who use their services has led to systematic biases in diagnostic processes, admission procedures and the provision of services.

There are also a number of ethical tensions that operate in medicine generally, and especially in psychiatry. The Hippocratic Oath (which is almost never taken by trainee doctors) states treatment will not be withheld from anyone, 'bond or free'. This has led to the development of the belief that medicine, and the provision of services, is value free, and that doctors treat illnesses regardless of race, colour or creed. Of course, this delightful vision is not true as any amount of sociological research on health care shows, but it remains a highly idealised tenet of medical practice. Doctors are reluctant to admit that it might not be true, and probably for this reason have resisted training in awareness of gender and ethnicity discrimination. It is therefore important to remember that few contemporary psychiatrists have had any training in anti-discriminatory practice and that they come from a different ethical tradition from those in the social sciences.

What psychiatrists do

As suggested above, psychiatrists assume a 'normal' state of mental health and are trained to identify abnormalities in that state. 'Normality' tends to be defined statistically and to some extent neurologically; there is a lot of emphasis in the psychiatric training on knowledge of brain function and brain disease. Contemporary Western psychiatry is still dualistic in approach, i.e. mind and body are seen as separate, while at the same time materialistic, i.e. the mind and the brain are the same. Hence the considerable research effort into the hypothesis that schizophrenia is a type of brain disease. Of course, it might be, but that would not necessarily provide any further information about what sufferers experience and what their needs are in terms of care.

> *Who in the rainbow can draw the line where the violet tint ends and the orange tint begins? Distinctly we see the difference of the colours, but where exactly does the one first blendingly enter into the other? So with sanity and insanity. In pronounced cases there is no question about them. But in some supposed cases, in various degrees supposedly less pronounced, to draw the exact line of demarcation few will undertake, though for a fee becoming considerate some professional experts will. There is nothing nameable, but that some men will, or undertake to, do it for pay.* (Herman Melville, 1924)

An alternative view came from Szasz (1962) when he said:

> *Psychiatrists are not concerned with mental illnesses and their treatment. In actual practice they deal with personal, social and ethical problems in living … human behaviour is fundamentally moral behaviour.*

Like any other health speciality, how psychiatric services are provided and resources made available is a political issue, which is influenced by the social discourses of the day. In Victorian times, the mentally ill were kept away from other people, often for many years. They were seen as both objects of pity and as evidence of deviance to be excluded from society. Psychiatry's role was to keep them apart; hence perhaps psychiatrists were then known also as 'alienists'. In contrast, by the 1960s, psychiatry was seen as an agent of social control, and there was a powerful social movement that was critical of psychiatric services, especially the old asylums. This led to the normalisation movement that pressed for the destigmatisation of mental disorder and the development of care in the community. The big asylums were closed, and emphasis was put on keeping people at home and looked after by community teams linked with GP services.

However, in the 1990s, psychiatrists were criticised for failing to be agents of social control. When homicides by mentally disordered patients became the subject of public attention, a social discourse grew up that assumed that the role of psychiatry was to stop psychiatric patients being a risk to others. Resources for secure inpatient beds were made available, and the number of secure inpatient units tripled. The management of patient risk is now accepted as being an essential part of mental health practice. What is particularly interesting about this social development is that the number of homicides by the mentally ill is the same as it has always been since records have been kept, i.e. about 100 per year. This figure should be compared with the 212 people killed at work through health and safety failure, the 200 people killed by accidents in the home and the 4,000 killed on the roads. The risk of being killed by someone with a mental illness is less than winning the lottery but the public representation in the media over the last 15 years does not reflect this.

Finally, there remains considerable debate about what is or is not a mental health problem. Homosexuality was a crime until the 1960s, then a psychiatric disorder until 1976. Another example is substance abuse. This is an ancient and widespread problem, going back thousands of years. Societies have always had to deal with addicts, and have tended to do so by a mixture of restricting supply and punishing those who deal in the substance. The number of addicts dependent on any substance in a society is affected by the availability of that substance within their community. This in turn depends on its legitimacy and price. Thus alcohol and nicotine addiction are much more widespread than cocaine addiction in the UK, but they are legitimate whereas cocaine is not. They also make a substantial contribution to the Exchequer and, indeed, many alcohol-producing companies are substantial contributors to party political funds. What is particularly striking about alcohol abuse is that it substantially increases the risk of violence by the mentally ill and is a potent risk factor for violence in its own right. If a government were serious about reducing risk in the community, it would make alcohol prohibitively expensive and ban those with a history of criminal law-breaking from drinking. However, this would not be socially acceptable or politically expedient; it is, however, socially acceptable apparently to encourage the print media to talk up the danger of violence by the mentally ill and chastise mental health professionals for failing to protect the public.

Mental state examination

The mental state examination (MSE) is the principal psychiatric tool, a semi-structured assessment covering: appearance, speech, mood, thought (form, content or stream), cognitive state and insight. Psychiatrists are taught to carry out the MSE as an essential part of their training. It is the combination of symptoms and signs which suggests diagnosis. No one aspect of the MSE alone is diagnostic. They should be considered as pieces of a jigsaw puzzle, which together with the patient's own account and information from others, may suggest a diagnosis. Of course they reflect cultural norms, so it is important to know what cultural norms are meaningful for the patient.

Appearance

This covers all aspects of the patient's appearance, including clothes, facial expression and a description of their demeanour. This does reflect a personal judgement, i.e. 'poorly dressed' should reflect something about the lack of appropriate clothes rather than a comment on style. People's clothing often does tell us something about their state of mind: are they dishevelled or dirty? Is the combination of clothes an odd one? What do others who know them think of their dress? Skin tone and colour is important: does this person look physically well or not? Do they look as though they have not slept? Older than their years? All these elements may suggest someone who is feeling very anxious. Facial expression is obvious: do they look worried or sad? Are they frowning, scowling, glaring? Are the eyebrows furrowed? All these may be pointers to the patient's subjective state, or alert the assessor to possibilities.

Speech

This covers all aspects of speech such as tone, volume and speed. Fluctuations in any of these may be noted, as well as whether the speaker leaves spaces for the assessor to speak. If not, this is called 'pressure of speech' and may indicate anxiety or, in more severe cases, manic illnesses. Its opposite, 'poverty of speech' may indicate low mood or thought disorder. Speech is often a reflection of thought processes.

Mood

Obvious highs and lows of mood are noted here, as well as irritability. Here the assessor should ask about physical signs of mood disorders: sleep disturbance, altered libido or appetite for food. The assessor should also ask about suicidal or homicidal ideas – these may be best expressed as gentle questions about a sense of hopelessness or fearfulness, which might give rise to thoughts of doing violence to self or to others rather than a bold 'Do you want to kill yourself?'

Thought

This is an opportunity to pursue hints of disturbance suggested by listening to the patient's speech. Here one is commenting on the *content* of what is said. This includes looking for evidence of delusional beliefs, i.e. beliefs held rigidly in the face of contrary evidence and which are culturally inappropriate for that person. Thus most religious beliefs do not figure here unless they involve the patient themselves being a supernatural figure.

The most important aspects to look for are those beliefs which involve other people or which involve the patient believing their personal inner world is being invaded. Such beliefs may contribute an increased risk of violence in certain circumstances. Any beliefs indicating fear or a sense of threat of persecution ('paranoid' beliefs) should be noted. Other beliefs to look for are those involving the patient's body, since these may indicate a mood disorder such as depression.

Assessment of thought involves assessing perception, especially whether a patient is suffering from hallucinations. It is better to ask, 'Have you been having any experiences that you can't explain or worry you?' than 'Do you hear voices?' Auditory hallucinations are most commonly seen in schizophrenia, but can also occur in mood disorders, and rarely in those with severe anxiety. Hallucinations in any other sense modality (touch, taste, smell or sight) are often associated with brain disease, especially epilepsy and, rarely, brain tumours. The presence of such hallucinations should prompt referral for neurological investigation. Hallucinations may sometimes be confused with sensory memories of previous experience and care needs to be taken to check this out.

Cognitive state

This is the part of the interview where basic orientation and consciousness is assessed. It is a crude exclusion procedure, since real cognitive tests of awareness and memory are more complicated than simple questions and answers can give. However, if the patient cannot tell you the day or date, does not know where they are or cannot register or recall small amounts of new information, it is likely that they have diminished awareness and the cause of this needs to be established. Clearly, if they are very elderly, dementia may be the most likely possibility, but physical illness or drug intoxication can produce similar symptoms and should always be considered.

Insight

This is a difficult area because it is fraught with potential for bias and prejudice. Basically, this part of the interview should assess what the patient makes of their current situation and its causes. It should also include the patient's responses to others' views of what is wrong. It should not simply be a statement of whether the patient agrees with the doctor or not that he or she is ill! However, it is not uncommon for patients to be deemed to have no insight because they do not accept that mental illness is the cause of their problems. Insight assessment is likely to be affected by the cultural and conceptual biases of the assessor and should never be used as the sole indicator of mental illness.

Other aspects of assessment and diagnosis

Assessment should begin with the history from the patient. It should include questions not only about the current problems but also about early childhood, especially details of parental care and attachments. 'Were you ever frightened of any adult when you were a child?' is a better question than 'Were you abused?' and allows discussion of which adult and why. It should be remembered that physical abuse and neglect of children is commoner than sexual abuse but just as bad for mental health. If the patient answers negatively to questions of childhood abuse, this should not be pursued.

It is also wise to ask about any history of being a victim of violence or crime in adulthood. Questions about contact with the criminal law may also be helpful. Diagnosis is a matter of summing up all the available evidence and suggesting the most likely candidates. Mental health teams should be prepared to be flexible in making diagnoses, since mental states can change in days. The person's whole story should contribute to diagnosis, not one symptom alone. However, it must be said that this is a counsel of perfection, and on Friday nights at midnight in casualty departments the labels given are not well thought out. The problem then is that they tend to stick.

Chapter 3
An overview of psychiatry and classification

There are two important distinctions in classical psychiatry: organic *vs* functional disorders and neurotic *vs* psychotic disorders. Although these distinctions may actually not be very robust, they are still widely used and taught and so they need some explanation.

Organic *vs* functional disorders

Psychiatric illness is divided loosely into *organic* and *functional* states. In organic states the mental disturbance is due to a detectable pathology which includes brain damage or injury, whereas in functional disorders there is no such damage detectable and the disorder is assumed to be a result of brain/mind dysfunction rather than damage. As some organic states are easily treatable, so psychiatric examination always emphasises the exclusion of organic brain disorders before any other diagnosis is made. However, they are comparatively rare in general psychiatric practice.

Organic states may be:

- due to a specific or generalised brain disorder;
- manifested as specific or general psychological symptoms;
- acute or chronic.

Those organic states that are reversible and treatable usually have an underlying infectious or biochemical cause. There are many causes of acute organic states:

- infections, e.g. HIV or meningitis;
- brain tumours (may be primary or secondary);
- intoxication with drugs (either prescribed or non-prescribed);
- poisoning;
- injury;
- vascular 'strokes'.

One of the cardinal symptoms of an acute organic state is confusion. The patient may also show signs of disorientation in terms of time and place and there may be memory disturbance. Acute organic disorders are often sudden in presentation and a sudden deterioration in mental state should alert one to the presence of an organic state. In contrast, chronic organic states tend to have a generalised cause and tend to present as more generalised psychological deterioration. Chronic organic states are also called 'dementia', and there are a number of different types.

The most well-known form of dementia is Alzheimer's disease, but there are many others, such as Korsakoff's disease caused by alcoholic brain damage and dementia caused by multiple small strokes ('multi-infarction/vascular dementia'). They result in gradual loss of brain tissue and associated gradual loss of mental functioning. There is no curative treatment for chronic dementing illness.

There are now medications that may slow down the process and give sufferers and their families an extension of normal life for a time, usually about 6–12 months. Sufferers and their carers need support and attention to both mental and physical needs. Once the dementing process has started, most patients tend to die within five or ten years.

Psychotic *vs* neurotic disorders

Psychotic states

These are those psychological states where there is altered perception of external reality. This most commonly takes the form of perceptions without external stimuli (hallucinations). Hallucinations occur in all sense modalities, but auditory hallucinations are the commonest in psychiatry. Hallucinations of taste and smell should alert one to the possibility of organic brain disease.

In addition to the perceptional disturbance, delusions may be present. Delusions are beliefs that are firmly held in the face of incontrovertible conflicting evidence and on the basis of apparently irrational or incoherent reasons, e.g. 'I know the CIA are at the bottom of my garden because the milk float arrived at five past seven instead of seven o'clock'. Delusions may or may not be true; it is the way that patients evaluate evidence that suggests a delusional process.

Psychotic states can occur in both organic and functional disorders, i.e. it is possible for those with brain disease or serious physical illnesses to be psychotic. Psychotic states may be caused by drug intoxication or misuse, as well as mental illnesses like schizophrenia or severe depression.

Neurotic states (anxiety spectrum disorders)

These, by definition, are those disorders where there is subjective distress (usually sadness or worry) but reality is preserved, i.e. there is no evidence of irrationally held beliefs or perceptions without stimuli. Neurotic states need to be distinguished from neurotic symptoms which are very common, whereas neurotic states are less so. However, it is thought that neurotic disorders have a prevalence of about 4 per cent in the community, representing a large amount of distress. Personality disorders are a type of neurotic state which will be discussed later.

The most common illnesses treated by psychiatrists are (in order): schizophrenia, affective disorders, chronic organic states, neurotic and personality disorders, substance misuse. In terms of prevalence, neurotic disorders and substance misuse are far more common in the general population than either schizophrenia or major affective disorder (MAD, i.e. either severe depression or manic states). It is usual for people to have more than one disorder (dual diagnosis): for example, many people with personality disorders also suffer from mood disorders and substance dependence.

Although it is commonly assumed that people have either psychotic conditions or neurotic conditions, in fact co-morbidity is commoner than previously thought. For example, people with severe personality disorders may also have brief psychotic episodes. Similarly, brief loss of contact with reality is not uncommon in both panic states and in prolonged depression. The classic psychotic states seen in psychiatry tend to be prolonged (weeks and months rather than days) and sufferers do not recover spontaneously.

Classification systems in psychiatry

The two systems which are used in Western psychiatry are:

- the **ICD** (the *International Classification of Diseases* – currently version 10), published by the World Health Organisation; and

- the **DSM** (the *Diagnostic and Statistical Manual* – currently version IV), published by the American Psychiatric Association.

The ICD is mainly used in Europe (including the UK) and the DSM is most commonly used in the USA, Australia and New Zealand. There are differences between the two systems.

ICD

The ICD offers a diagnostic labelling system, with guidelines for making a definite diagnosis and instructions about inclusion and exclusion. For example, the features of 'acute schizophrenia-like psychotic disorder' are described in one paragraph, and three guidelines are given for a definite diagnosis. Five other psychotic disorders are included as diagnostic possibilities and two are excluded. The assessor decides which of the labels best describes the patient. There are ten main categories used in ICD10:

F0   Organic, including symptomatic, mental disorders

F1   Mental and behaviour disorders due to psychoactive substance abuse

F2   Schizophrenia, schizotypal and delusional disorders

F3   Mood (affective) disorders

F4   Neurotic, stress-related and somatoform disorders

F5   Behavioural syndromes associated with physiological disturbances and physical factors

F6   Disorders of adult personality and behaviour

F7   Mental retardation

F8   Disorders of psychological development

F9   Behavioural and emotional disorders, onset usually occurring in childhood or adolescence

ICD–11 is planned for 2015.

DSM

The DSM, in contrast, uses an operational system. Diagnosis cannot be made unless a patient meets a number of criteria. In addition, mental functioning is assessed on four different axes:

- Axis 1 covers general mental health.
- Axis 2 covers personality function.
- Axis 3 covers neurological health.
- Axis 4 covers general (physical) health status.

In both cases, the diagnostic systems are based on epidemiological research and committees of psychiatrists decide what needs to be included or excluded. On the principle that you get out what you put in, it is clear that there is enormous potential for bias in the system. The best example of this is the inclusion of homosexuality in the DSM until an organised protest caused it to be removed in the early 1970s. In the ICD, it states that *sexual orientation alone is not to be regarded as a disorder*, although it is possible to code homosexuality under F66.x1 if it is thought that this is *problematic for the individual*.

Other criticisms of the DSM include the concern that it may reflect sexist and racist stereotypes. However, on balance, the DSM is to be preferred. The operational criteria tend to reduce the tendency of clinicians to apply diagnoses casually and offer the opportunity of reviewing the diagnosis. It is also useful for research purposes, improving consistency between researchers. However, neither system can protect a patient against sloppy or negligent clinical practice.

DSM version V is expected in May 2012.

Chapter 4
Psychotic disorders

There are four main psychotic states:

- schizophrenia;

- affective psychoses;

- paranoid states;

- post-natal illnesses.

These will be discussed in turn.

Schizophrenia

This is probably a collection of illnesses rather than a single entity. There has been much discussion about the validity of the diagnosis. Surveys suggest that a syndrome like schizophrenia can be found in most countries, although the incidence can vary tremendously, e.g. there is a much higher incidence in Sweden than in the Hutterite population of America. In addition the progress of schizophrenia seems to be better in Third World countries than in Western countries. The prevalence of schizophrenia is about 1 per cent but it seems that the incidence of schizophrenia is actually falling.

Symptoms and progress of the illness

Schizophrenia may be acute or chronic. It appears that the disease has a relapsing, fluctuating nature with acute periods followed by periods of chronicity, usually with a drop in social and cognitive functioning. The key symptom is *disorder of thought*. In addition there are *disorders of perception* such as hallucinations. Schizophrenics also suffer from a number of other psychotic phenomena, e.g. delusion, certain thought insertion and withdrawal and passivity feelings. In chronic presentation, schizophrenia is characterised by thought disorder, under-activity, withdrawal, self-neglect and apathy. Without treatment the patient will continue to deteriorate in social and mental functioning over a long period of time.

Diagnosis

In the UK a diagnosis of schizophrenia must be made in the absence of organic brain disease. Historically, a diagnosis of schizophrenia was based on the presence of one or more of Schneider's first rank symptoms:

- delusions;

- hallucination, mostly third-person auditory hallucination;

- delusions of thought control: insertion withdrawal;

- passivity feeling, i.e. belief one's movements are controlled by external forces.

In DSM IV there is a requirement that these symptoms should have persisted for at least six months before the diagnosis is made, and although ICD10 requires symptoms to be present for only one month there must be a concomitant decline in social functioning and personality

Aetiology

The cause of schizophrenia is unknown. Genetic and familial studies suggest that there is a strong genetic component, and some Scandinavian studies have suggested the involvement of chromosome 5. However, these have not been replicated elsewhere. Nevertheless, there is no doubt that there is a genetic component to some of the manifestations of schizophrenia.

Other possible theories include:

- perinatal birth injury/brain damage;

- viral infection (because of excess of births in the spring);

- poor emotional regulation, e.g. high expressed emotion appears to provoke relapse;

- biochemical disorders, e.g. dopamine excess in the fronto-temporal regions of the brain;

- structural abnormalities in fronto-temporal lobes of brain or in the limbic system (amygdala).

Of the above theories, the dopamine hypothesis has the most support and treatment is based on that hypothesis. However, current theories need to explain why schizophrenia is over-represented among people of low socio-economic class and why 40 per cent of those who are identical twins do not develop schizophrenia, although their twins do.

Treatment

Treatment is largely symptomatic, i.e. drugs are prescribed to remove the symptoms rather than treat any underlying cause. Schizophrenics also need psychological and social support and rehabilitation if they have been ill for some years. Problems include avoiding institutionalisation and the side-effects of long-term neuroleptic medication.

Affective psychoses

Affective psychoses are disorders of *mood*. These are severe types of affective disorder with psychotic features which may present as either depression or mania. In youth it may often present as mania while in old age depression is a more common presentation of an affective disorder. It is important to remember irritability may be either a sign of depression or mania. Depression is common in the elderly and needs to be kept in mind as a likely problem.

Symptoms, presentation and progress

- *Appearance* – may look depressed or elated. May show psychomotor retardation or may appear to be very restless and hyperactive. Look for decreased eye contact.

- *Speech* – if depressed, will usually be monosyllabic or mute; if manic there will be pressure of speech and the patient will be so garrulous it may be impossible to communicate with them.

- *Mood* – any questions about mood will reveal depression or elation. Ask about disturbances of sleep, appetite and weight. Ask about suicide/homicide thought; thought disorder will rarely be prominent, although it may present in manic patients.

- *Delusions and hallucinations* – will reflect mood, i.e. manic patients will be grandiose and often have religious delusions, while depressed patients may have delusions of guilt, doom and ill health. Both types of patient may have persecutory delusions and may therefore be hyper-aroused. Delusions of thought control and passivity feelings are rare.

- *Cognition* – may be disorientated especially if depression is severe. In the early stages depression may resemble dementia.

- *Insight* – is usually absent if a patient is psychotic.

Schizo-affective psychosis is a term coined to cover patients with essentially a schizophrenic picture who also have pronounced affective features. Generally the course of the disease is more like a depressive illness in that the response to treatment is better. Recent research in this area suggests that affective psychosis and schizophrenia are more alike than previously thought.

The chief risk of any affective disorder is that of suicide. Homicide followed by suicide is also known, especially in women with severe depression and men separated from their families.

Aetiology

Genetic and familial studies suggest that affective disorder has a strong genetic component. Swedish studies suggest that the gene for bipolar affective disorder is likely to be located on chromosome 4. The genetic/familial association seems to be stronger for the severe psychotic affective disorders rather than for neurotic disorders. It is probable that the genetic risk relates to genes for the production of chemicals responsible for mood regulation in the brain.

Other possible theories include:

- low levels of monoamines or hormones in the brain;
- the role of life events and stress;
- the role of negative thoughts and how thoughts and mood are related;
- early childhood experiences of loss, separation and hostility.

The monoamine theory of depression currently has most currency and is the rationale for anti-depressant treatment.

Treatment

This can include: anti-depressant medication, anti-psychotic medication, ECT (electro-convulsive therapy) and psychotherapy.

See Chapter 11 for more information on psychiatric treatments.

See Chapters 12–16 which provide more detail on the use of psychiatric medication in treatment.

Paranoid states

Distinguish:

- paranoid symptoms;
- paranoid personality disorder;
- paranoid syndromes.

The word 'paranoid' literally means 'beside one's self', and is actually therefore a rather general term. It has come to mean any psychological experience involving another person and has also come to be used interchangeably with 'persecutory'. Although it is true that most paranoid experiences involve persecutory thoughts and beliefs about another person, they may also involve very positive attachments to another person. The fact that they are positive in nature, however, is potentially misleading: these are psychotic attachments and therefore both irrational and unstable in nature.

Paranoid symptoms

Paranoid symptoms are quite common in the general population, and especially common in alcohol intoxication (hence the fateful question, 'Are you looking at me?'). If persistent, they may indicate the presence of schizophrenia, affective disorders, paranoid personality disorder and many organic states.

Paranoid personality disorder

Paranoid personality disorder is a chronic disorder of mood, thought and behaviour in which the individual is hostile, tetchy and suspicious of others. Generally this has been noted from childhood or early adolescence and marks the individual out as 'unusual'. For such people a theme of persecution dominates and pervades their entire life and they are often isolated figures. It is highly treatment resistant and if the individual turns to violence as a result they may be extremely dangerous.

Paranoid syndromes

Isolated and encapsulated paranoid beliefs occur in the absence of other symptoms of schizophrenic or affective disorder. This has been particularly noted in the elderly living alone with a sensory deficit. It has also been noted in men and women who develop positive but pathological attachments to famous figures (so called 'erotomania'). A further example of a paranoid syndrome is pathological jealousy. These syndromes may give rise to stalking behaviours and, rarely, violence.

Post-natal disorders

Post-natal psychosis is only one type of maternal psychiatric condition and not the commonest. However, it is convenient to discuss it with the other post-natal disorders. These can be divided as follows.

Maternity 'blues'

This presents as tearfulness and slight confusion or agitation which occurs in the first week after childbirth, usually on day two or three. This is extremely common, and probably reflects hormonal imbalance immediately post-partum. It usually resolves spontaneously; if there is prolonged sadness or tearfulness then this may indicate the development of a post-partum psychosis.

Post-partum psychosis

This occurs in the second or third week after childbirth. It is almost certainly of organic origin and generally presents as an affective psychosis. It is dangerous because of the risk to both mother and baby. It responds well to treatment. It occurs in 1 in 500 births. There is an increased risk if there has been previous post-partum psychosis or if there is a positive family history.

Post-natal depression

This occurs usually around the third month after birth and a small number may not manifest until a year after childbirth. It seems to be related to psychological and social factors, especially lack of social supports. It can be highly persistent and has a damaging effect on child rearing and women's general health.

Chapter 5
Neurotic disorders, substance abuse and personality disorders

Neurotic disorders

The word neurosis derives from the Greek word for nerve. It has come to mean mild psychiatric morbidity. The definition of a neurotic disorder is *the experience of mental distress where reality is preserved*. In practice, this means the experience of anxiety or sadness which is enough to impair functioning.

Demographic data

Neurotic symptoms are common. A study in Manhattan suggests that 80 per cent of the population suffered from neurotic symptoms but probably a truer figure is between 15 and 20 per cent. Nearly everyone experiences neurotic symptoms at some time, and most people will manage these without seeking professional help.

Neurotic disorders are the commonest form of psychiatric illness. However, the majority of sufferers are not seen by psychiatric services but are managed by primary care services and the voluntary sector. Neurotic disorders are said to form the bulk of GP work and GPs manage mild depression and anxiety disorders using medication and short-term psychological therapies. Neurotic disorders affect twice as many women as men, although this may reflect women's greater ability to seek help when distressed. It seems that marriage is protective for men but can make women more vulnerable to neurotic symptoms. Neurotic disorders are commoner in urban areas and commonly coexist with substance misuse.

There are three main types of neurotic disorder: anxiety disorders, depression and mixed. In practice, those who are depressed are also anxious and vice versa. It may be better to think about whether the distress is focused on one particular experience or event or is more generalised.

Anxiety disorders

These include:

- generalised anxiety disorder;

- phobic disorders;

- panic disorders;
- obsessive–compulsive disorder;
- somatisation disorder (hypochondriasis);
- post-traumatic stress disorder (PTSD).

The latter may be generalised anxiety at a high or low level. Some people are characteristically anxious. Anxiety is biologically life preserving in that it increases arousal. It is probably best to see it on a continuum with fear and rage as the other extreme.

The definition of an anxiety state is *a sense of threat to no perceived stimulus* (cf. *fear which is the sense of threat to a perceived stimulus*).

The sensation of anxiety is extremely unpleasant. It takes the form of multiple physical and psychological symptoms such as headache, nausea, fainting, chest tightness, shortness of breath, tingling in the hands and fingers, etc.

Phobic disorders
This is severe anxiety/panic associated with some specific stimulus, such as enclosed spaces or animals. Agoraphobia is a fear of going outside, and is commonly associated with depression and PTSD. Phobias are easily treated with behavioural therapy.

Panic disorders
These are increased attacks of panic or risk of attack to no particular stimulus. Panic attacks can occur with unexpected suddenness in any situation.

Obsessive–compulsive disorder
This is a distressing condition. The patient experiences intrusive, persistent thoughts he or she cannot get out of their mind. These are alien and often unpleasant, but recognised by the patient as his/her thoughts. These thoughts may cause anxiety in themselves which lead to the formation of compulsive rituals which may be time-consuming and destructive, e.g. a patient with persistent thoughts that he/she is contaminated by dirt from the outside world may develop compulsive rituals of hand washing even knowing this to be a fear without foundation. Obsessives may suffer from violent thoughts but almost never act on them. Obsessive–compulsive disorder is rare and usually responds to treatment except in cases where the condition has gone on for such a long time that it becomes resistant to treatment.

Somatisation disorder (previously called hypochondriasis)
The patient has a persistent belief they are suffering from illness or interprets minor physical sensations as evidence of major physical illness. They may present with multiple unexplained medical symptoms and have multiple investigations all to no avail. Patients find it hard to accept reassurance and often persist in obtaining different medical opinions. This in turn produces anxiety and depression which reduce the patient's abilities to tolerate stress and pain. Anxiety itself can produce physical symptoms, so it is not surprising that psychological/physical symptoms tend to interact. Often such patients are very intolerant of psychological distress, seeming to prefer to be physically 'ill'. This disorder is commonly seen in general practice.

Post-traumatic stress disorder (PTSD)

This is a mental illness which occurs in about 20–30 per cent of people who survive or witness or assist in a disaster or major trauma. After trauma, the majority of people will experience distress, disturbed sleep and nightmares. However, most people make a natural recovery from these symptoms over the course of 6–12 months. In a small proportion of people, symptoms persist and become disabling. Such individuals may develop chronic nightmares, flashbacks and intrusive memories of the trauma. They tend to avoid any reminders of the trauma and this can have a profound impact on other aspects of their lives. Substance abuse is common in patients with PTSD, as is depression. PTSD is more likely after personal traumas such as crime, and where people experienced great fear or believed they were going to die. PTSD is common in psychiatric populations, many of whom have been victimised in various ways, and should be looked for. Treatment involves medication and carefully regulated memory work, which should only be done by psychologists and psychotherapists with expertise in this area. This is especially true for childhood trauma. Chronic PTSD is hard to treat, so giving people support early may be helpful.

Mood disorders

Another term for these disorders is neurotic depression, which is seen as the milder end of the scale from a psychotic depression. Depression is much commoner in women and is associated with a number of vulnerability factors:

- living in a poor area;
- three children under the age of 10;
- loss of the mother before the age of 11;
- lack of a confiding relationship.

Neurotic depression may also be mixed with anxiety and there is some debate about whether anxiety and depression are two discrete entities.

Depression which is severe enough to impair function but not usually sufficiently bad to warrant referral to psychiatric services is commonly caused or triggered by life events, such as trauma and bereavement. Divorce, bereavement and moving house are the most potent causes of life stress and some people will develop depression after such events.

Miscellaneous neurotic conditions

Hysterical phenomena

Hysteria was thought originally to apply only to women and in some senses developed as a pejorative term. It also sometimes used to mean histrionic in the sense of overacting. The true definition is *the restriction of physical function, including consciousness, arising from repressed psychic distress*. It is not clear how common hysterical phenomena are; if diagnosed in a general hospital they often turn out to have underlying organic illness, but if diagnosed in a psychiatric hospital the diagnosis is probably true. They may be difficult to treat because of the powerful negative reinforcing effect of experiencing distress.

Altered consciousness has been associated with: fugue states which involve wandering and amnesia; loss of personal identity states; multiple personality disorder. An interesting development has been in the understanding of the impact of psychological trauma on consciousness. It is possible that those who have been traumatised have lapses of conscious awareness – what is called 'dissociation'. Dissociation tends to happen at times of stress and it may be that hysteria is a form of chronic dissociative state.

Eating disorders
These may be divided into:

- anorexia nervosa;

- bulimia;

- mixed syndromes.

Most commonly found in young women, anorexia nervosa may be understood as a phobia about being fat and an addiction to not eating. It has a poor prognosis, especially if it starts young, and it carries a substantial mortality risk. It appears to be increasing in incidence. Bulimia includes both self-starvation and gorging behaviour and appears to be commoner than anorexia. As a syndrome, it may be combined with substance abuse and deliberate self-harm.

How do neuroses arise?

There are many different theories proposed to account for the mechanisms of neurotic disorders but they fall roughly into three groups.

- *Biological:*
  - genetic defects;
  - defect in neurological systems (e.g. hypersensitivity of nerve ends);
  - neuro-transmitter excess or deficit: especially 5-HT arousal systems;
  - associated with hormonal changes;
  - brain damage (e.g. increased neurotic symptoms after minor head injury).

- *Psychological:*
  - defects in bonding and attachment with maternal figures (Bowlby, 1973);
  - defects in learning patterns and in recognising threat;
  - temperamental traits reinforced by rearing (Thomas and Chess, 1977);
  - psychodynamic theory – this proposes that neurotic symptoms are a defence against childhood anxiety and represent fixation at a childhood level of psychological development. Thus neuroses were protective in childhood but maladaptive in adulthood.

- *Socio-environmental.* Ill health is a political issue and mental health is no exception. Theories of neurosis need to explain the increased levels of neurosis in urban areas, women and lower socio-economic class. Possible factors involved might be:

- society's constructions of masculinity and femininity;

- culturally allowed expressions of dissent and unhappiness;

- validation of the illness role in this culture rather than role of political dissident;

- the financial implications of improving health in general;

- to be ill is one way of getting your needs acknowledged;

- poor schooling and education combine with any biological or psychological problem to interact and make matters worse;

- lack of social structure and social cohesion in current society.

In practice, it is likely that all three types of mechanism are at work. For example, genetically vulnerable individuals may be exposed to psychological risk through their early childhood experience. As a result of these risk factors, they may be more at risk of living in the type of environment that may trigger neurotic disorders.

Substance abuse

Addiction to substances has been known since ancient times. Substances of misuse and addiction tend to be those that relieve anxiety and distress or that elevate mood. Any substance that relieves anxiety may become misused: hence nicotine, chocolate and non-prescription painkillers are all known to be capable of misuse and addiction. The process whereby people become addicted is not well understood; it is likely to be a mixture of genetic vulnerability and environmental context. The genetic link is inferred from the fact that addiction tends to run in families; it may be that what is inherited is hyperarousal to stress or decreased stress reduction responses. There are powerful environmental risk factors; some occupations are well known for substance misuse risk such as the armed services, the entertainment and hospitality business, and health care professionals. Some types of illegal drug misuse are closely associated with belonging to a group of fellow misusers; this is common in young socially impoverished users.

An important theory in substance misuse is the 'self-medication hypothesis'. This suggests that addicts misuse the substance that best relieves their underlying psychological distress. Thus those with chronic depression take drugs like cocaine; those with chronic anxiety take drugs like alcohol and heroin. This theory applies well to those who develop substance misuse after traumatic experiences, which is extremely common, and where it is clear that individuals are using substances to manage their PTSD symptoms.

The commonest substance misuse problem in the UK, and the most problematic, is alcohol. It is problematic because of its association with risk: risk of serious accident and risk of violence. In the mentally disordered, the presence of substance misuse increases the risk of violence by a factor of 8 in the UK. There are thought to be 4 million alcoholics in England and Wales, i.e. people who have severe mental or physical damage due to alcohol. Fifty per cent of casualty admissions are alcohol related and a third of medical beds are used by those who have alcohol-related illnesses. Alcohol-related disorders also take their toll on the road and in the workplace.

The WHO definition of *alcohol dependency syndrome* includes:

- a feeling of being compelled to drink;
- stereotype pattern of drinking;
- altered tolerance to alcohol;
- withdrawal symptoms;
- primacy of drinking over other activities;
- drinking to avoid withdrawal symptoms.

The Royal College of Psychiatrists suggests a 'safe' level of alcohol is 21 units a week for men and 14 units a week for women. However, it is clear one could still be an addict even if drinking small amounts if one had no choice about whether one drank 21 units. It is likely many people in this country are addicted to alcohol in that they drink every single day and have done so for many years. Eventually, it becomes impossible to tell whether they are drinking from choice or from addiction.

Abuse of illicit substances also can cause physical and psychological harm, but the problem is still not on as large a scale as that of alcohol. Illicit drug use is less of a problem alone but is frequently combined with alcohol abuse – the problem of 'co-morbidity'. Addicts may also suffer from coexistent mental illness such as depression and schizophrenia. There is some reason to think that abusing drugs makes severe mental illnesses worse and makes relapse more likely.

Personality disorders

For many years, it was thought that this was a term which was used in so many different ways, including pejoratively of difficult patients, that it was without meaning. However, there is good evidence to think that disorders of personality do exist and can benefit from treatment.

Does a normal personality exist?

There are two ways to think about 'normal' personalities: 'normal' for the individual and 'normal' for their social context. For example, at one time, for a person to have a religious vocation and join an enclosed community was thought to be both a normal aspect of that individual's life and normal for their social and cultural group. Nowadays in the UK, entering a closed religious community may be seen as normal by an individual doing so but highly abnormal within most cultural groups, or at least regarded as unusual in a way that it used not to be.

This example shows the problems associated with classifying personality on the basis of behaviour and actions. From antiquity, it has been assumed that a man's character can be inferred from his behaviour, so that 'normal' personality is associated with 'normal' behaviour. However, normal behaviour is determined by many factors, most of which are not related to an individual's personality. Behaviour may be unusual but not abnormal: Mother Theresa's behaviour in Calcutta was highly unusual but not evidence of personality disorder (unless deviation from a statistical norm is evidence of disorder). This example also shows that when classifying personalities on the basis of behaviour, there is a tendency to focus only on negative or anti-social behaviours, which is misleading and unbalanced.

So what is personality? There are a number of ways to think about this. One might think of it in terms of character or self-defined identity. In the past, attempts to define personality have been in terms of character *types* or collections of *traits*. In ancient Greece, people might be defined in terms of their humour type: green or damp or melancholy. Trait theory suggests that the personality is made up of components, some of which are more dominant than others, such as extraversion or introversion.

More recently, there has been interest in the possibility of dimensions of personality, so that those with personality disorders have too much or too little of different kinds of traits, or perhaps exercise them differently at different times. Another way of thinking about personality is to think of it as the sum total of all the beliefs, values and attitudes with which we see the world. However, some of these values and attitudes can change with time, and so personality is a mixture of core beliefs and attitudes, and ways of interacting with others that are more flexible and can change. A normal personality may be understood as a 'socially functional personality' with the following features:

- some degree of consistency over time and different situations;
- recognisable to the individual and others;
- somewhat predictable;
- present since childhood;
- some acknowledgement of other people's rights in society.

On this account, personality disorders are those sets of negative beliefs, values and attitudes that cause social dysfunction for the individual and those around them. There are degrees of personality disorder: mild, moderate and severe, depending on the amount of social damage that is taking place. It is also possible for a person to become personality disordered after a traumatic experience. The diagnosis is not usually made until the person is 18, and any behavioural features of the personality disorder should be present from childhood.

Most of the ICD and DSM diagnostic systems for personality disorder still emphasise behaviour as a proxy for values and attitudes. Using DSM III-R, there are three clusters of personality disorder: schizoid, avoidant and flamboyant. The schizoid group tend to have diminished contact with reality and have extensive fantasy lives. It is thought that this group may be at increased risk for schizophrenia. The avoidant group have difficulty relating to others socially and withdraw; they rarely cause difficulties for others. The 'flamboyant' group do have significant problems with other people, and it is this group that most mental health care professionals will meet. The behaviours that cause most problems are criminal rule-breaking, social rule-breaking in terms of health care or employment, and family rule-breaking.

A key feature of personality disorder is that the individuals who have it do not manage distress and anxiety well. They suffer from subjective distress; it is just that they manage it either by withdrawing from others (and are therefore not seen by health care professionals) or by engaging with others in ways that alienate or alarm. It has been said of people with personality disorders that they do not know how to get effective care from others. Such patients seek help, but then find the model of care on offer hard to use. This leads to their rejection of care, which angers and alienates health carers who reject in their turn. This rejection is even more likely if the patient rejects what can be offered with displays of anger or self-harm.

Personality disorder may coexist with mental illness and frequently does. Young people with personality disorders are at increased risk of developing a major mental illness, and if they do this will make the personality disorder worse. People with personality disorders also are at increased risk of misusing substances and frequently have both these diagnoses.

Causes of personality disorder

One of the key features of personality disorder is an inability to manage negative emotions and arousal. The capacity to manage distress is a function of both genetic profile and early childhood experience. There is some evidence that genetic risk interacts with childhood adversity to cause ASPD (see below). There is good evidence that childhood abuse and neglect significantly increase the chance of developing a personality disorder in adulthood; this is especially true for neglect. Physical abuse and neglect may have more of a link with ASPD; sexual abuse in childhood increases the risk of developing BPD and depression (see below).

Although unusual, the experience of trauma in adulthood can also cause personality disorder, i.e. the experience of trauma damages the previously ordered personality organisation, probably by its effect on arousal and mood regulation.

Personality disorders in psychiatric practice

The prevalence of personality disorder in the community is about 10 per cent, i.e. at any one time about 10 per cent of the population suffer from a personality disorder. However, in psychiatric outpatients, the prevalence is about 30 per cent, and among inpatients about 50 per cent. In forensic settings (which offer services to those who have broken the criminal law), unsurprisingly the prevalence is about 70 per cent.

The commonest types of personality disorder seen in psychiatric practice are:

- anti-social personality disorder (ASPD – also known as dissocial or sociopathy);
- borderline personality disorder (BPD); and
- narcissistic personality disorder (NPD).

ASPD is diagnosed more frequently in males and BPD in females, but this may be an artefact of settings where patients are admitted. Both ASPD and BPD are associated with substance misuse; BPD is associated with mood disorders also. The prevalence of ASPD in the general population is about 4 per cent; for BPD it is about 2 per cent. These are therefore not common conditions in general, but considerably more common than schizophrenia (which takes up most of psychiatry's resources).

Anti-social personality disorder

It is important to distinguish three uses of almost synonymous terms:

- anti-social personality disorder – psychiatric term;

- psychopathic disorder – legal term used in the Mental Health Act 1983 until 2008;

- psychopath – used only in a lay sense.

Not everyone who was detained under the category of psychopathic disorder had a personality disorder or is a 'psychopath' in any proper sense of the word. The Mental Health Act term was a measure for detaining people with personality disorders who are aggressive; no patient detained under this category should be called a 'psychopath'. As from 2008 the term disappears for new detentions.

Most of the early writing on anti-social personality was somewhat anecdotal. Peter Scott identified four common themes in these terms: the exclusion of psychotic illness or sub-normality; the disorder is persistent from an early age; they suffer from abnormally aggressive behaviour; society is impelled to deal with such individuals. ASPD is a term most often used of violent young men. There is considerable overlap with criminal young men which is not surprising since a defining criterion is criminality. It is a term which could be used more in women; it is also possibly under-diagnosed in black populations.

The diagnosis of ASPD rests on having four of the following behaviours:

- sustains inconsistent work behaviour, as indicated by any of the following (including similar behaviour in academic settings if the person is a student):

  - unemployment for six months or more within five years when work was available;

  - repeated absences from work unexplained by illness in self or family;

  - abandonment of several jobs without realistic plans for others;

- fails to conform to social norms with respect to lawful behaviour, as indicated by repeat-edly performing anti-social acts that are grounds for arrest (whether arrested or not), e.g. destroying property, harassing others, stealing, pursuing an illegal occupation;

- is irritable and aggressive, as indicated by repeated physical fights or assaults (not required by one's job or to defend someone or oneself) including spouse- or child-beating;

- repeatedly fails to honour financial obligations, as indicated by defaulting on debts or failing to provide child support or support for other dependants on a regular basis;

- fails to plan ahead or is impulsive.

In addition three or more of the following should be present:

- was often truant;

- ran away from home overnight at least twice while living in parental home;

- often initiated physical fights;

- used a weapon in more than one fight;

- forced someone into sexual activity with him/her;
- was physically cruel to animals;
- was physically cruel to other people;
- deliberately destroyed others' property (other than fire-setting);
- deliberately engaged in fire-setting;
- often lied (other than to avoid physical or sexual abuse);
- has stolen without confrontation from a victim on more than one occasion (including forgery);
- stole with confrontation of victim (e.g. mugging, purse-snatching, extortion, armed robbery).

This emphasis on behaviour has made it difficult to distinguish ordinary criminals from ASPD. There is a subset of anti-social men and women who have been classified as 'psychopaths' using a system defined by Robert Hare. This has the advantage of using interpersonal attitudes and values as well as behaviours to make the classification. Hare psychopathy is rated using the Psychopathy Checklist – Revised (PCL-R V2), but is of little utility outside forensic settings. Most men and women with ASPD will be found in either prison or secure psychiatric settings.

Borderline personality disorder

Borderline personality disorder (BPD) is a term which has grown in its use over the last ten years. The 'borderline' referred to is that between neurosis and psychosis, and one of the diagnostic criteria for BPD is the presence of what are called 'micro psychotic episodes' in which patients lose contact with reality for short periods. They describe hallucinations and a sense of unreality and confusion; it is likely that they have altered consciousness at such times.

BPD is also associated with severe fluctuations in mood and instability of relationships, so that patients form intense connections to others which are then abandoned. BPD is a diagnosis most commonly used of women but it is probably under-diagnosed in men because of gender role stereotyping. Research suggests that BPD is possibly caused by, or understood as, a reaction to prolonged and severe child abuse, physical and/or sexual.

Narcissistic personality disorder

These individuals probably most closely resemble those who we call psychopaths. These are people who seem to have little empathy for others and do not respond to their concerns. If this is not combined with criminality then NPD patients may be unpopular but not necessarily ineffective; it is arguable that NPD traits are useful for some types of powerful positions in society, and if combined with intelligence and charm, those with NPD may be very successful. However, combined with sadistic tendencies or other types of violence, NPD is dangerous.

There is further discussion on 'psychopathic disorder' in Chapter 8 in the consideration of risk assessment and risk management.

Risk and personality disorder

The vast majority of people with personality disorders pose no threat to anyone but themselves. However, as will be clear from the above, there is a small group of individuals with ASPD, BPD and NPD who are violent to others and whose risk persists because of entrenched anti-social attitudes and beliefs.

After the murder of a woman and her daughter by a man with ASPD, the government has attempted to develop a strategy for managing people with personality disorders who are dangerous. The Home Office and Department of Health paper *Managing Dangerous People with Severe Personality Disorder*, published in 1999, stated:

> *Personality disorder is a term used to describe a number of different conditions. The great majority of people with personality disorder cause at most some distress to themselves or to their family or friends – for example by their obsessive or compulsive behaviour. But at the other end of the spectrum is a small group of people who are very seriously disordered and who pose a very high risk to the public. This paper is concerned with the problems presented by this small group. There are estimated to be just over 2,000 people who would fall into this group in England and Wales. Over 98% of these people are men, and at any time most are in prison or in secure hospitals. But the law as it stands fails to protect the public from the danger these people represent because in many cases they have to be allowed to return to the community even though they remain dangerous … Research into the causes of severe personality disorder, and into how best to address the associated risks, has been inconclusive. New research has been commissioned but will take time to complete. Decisions on the direction of policy development for managing this group cannot be delayed until the outcomes of the research are known.*

A White Paper on mental health law reform suggested that dangerous people with severe personality disorders would be included within a new Mental Health Act and legislation would allow for indefinite detention without treatment for those who seemed dangerous. Massive and united professional opposition caused the government to drop this proposal. The 2007 Act tackled the issue by having a very inclusive definition of 'mental disorder' and by replacing the 'treatability test' with a test as to whether 'appropriate' treatment is available.

Summary

Personality disorder is still used to describe difficult patients – mainly because it takes too long to say 'This is a person who behaves in a horrid way, but it's not entirely their fault; on the other hand, they are not ill either.' Some personality disorders do respond to treatment – always of the psycho-therapeutic kind and probably nearly always in a group situation. This neatly reflects the involvement of both internal and external factors in the development of personality and the need to assess both in difficult clients. It is no longer true to say that personality disorder is untreatable, only that services that could treat it may not be available.

Chapter 6
Forensic psychiatry

In this chapter we discuss how psychiatrists relate to those who break the criminal law and who may pose a real threat to others as a result of their mental illness. There is further discussion about risk in Chapter 8, but given the current emphasis on risk management in psychiatry it is useful to review psychiatry's involvement with criminal offenders.

Definition of forensic psychiatry

Forensic psychiatry is the study and care of mentally abnormal offenders, i.e. those who have committed offences as a result of mental illness. In addition 'challenging' behaviours may be assessed and dealt with. The work divides into three areas:

- *Justice* – court reports: pre-trial and post-trial; appearances in court as an expert witness.
- *Community* – liaison with other psychiatric specialities; consultation services; outpatient and domiciliary services; liaison with probation officers and social services, GPs, etc.
- *Inpatient work* – close supervision units or locked wards; medium-security units; high-security hospitals, e.g. Broadmoor.

Generally speaking, forensic psychiatry is no different from general psychiatry. Assessments are made of the patients, histories taken and diagnoses made. Treatment may be in the form of biological strategies such as drugs, psychological strategies such as psychotherapy, or sociological changes such as improvements in housing. This approach is the same whether the patient is in the community or an inpatient although work in prisons is necessarily hampered by prison systems.

What is particular is the patient group. The vast majority of forensic patients are young and male. They come from socially impoverished backgrounds, full of risk factors for both physical and mental health. They are more likely than ordinary patients to have been exposed to child abuse and neglect, to have been in care and to have a personality disorder. They rarely have completed basic education, rarely have good employment histories and rarely enjoy family support. Women patients are unusual, because violent women are unusual in every culture. However, when women are violent and dangerous they are similar to their male counterparts.

The Reed Report (Department of Health and Home Office, 1992) suggested that the care of mentally disordered offenders should take place:

- with regard to quality of care and proper attention to individual need;
- with regard to their rights as citizens;

Mental disorders and violence

The vast majority of violent acts are carried out by people who are mentally well, although they may be temporarily highly distressed or aroused. The commonest type of violence in the UK is fighting between young men who are drunk. The second commonest is domestic violence in the home.

Violent behaviour is in fact quite rare, in terms of criminality. The commonest type of crime is theft and property damage; violence only accounts for 6 per cent of recorded crime. Even if this is an underestimate, violence would still be an unusual type of behaviour. Furthermore, since most violent offenders are not mentally ill, it can easily be understood why the risk of a mentally ill person acting violently is tiny.

This having been said, it is established that there are some types of abnormal mental states which increase the risk of violence. Any type of paranoid state or symptom carries an increased risk of violence. Hallucinations of an intrusive type, e.g. of having thoughts inserted or removed, increase the risk. Alcohol dependence is a risk factor for violence. If a patient with paranoid psychotic symptoms also has an anti-social personality disorder and a substance misuse problem, this increases the risk of violence dramatically.

The main reason that homicides by the mentally ill continue to occur, despite increased risk management and supervision, is that when a mentally ill person acts violently, he or she does so in an unpredictable way. The mentally disordered are dangerous because their violence is unpredictable, not because it is likely. As stated earlier, the rate of homicide by the mentally ill has not altered in 30 years, and specifically has not altered in the last ten years, despite enhanced supervision and risk management strategies.

Forensic psychiatry and the interface with the law

Forensic psychiatry's involvement with the law stems from the long-held belief that if one commits a criminal act when mentally ill, one should not be held responsible for that act and thus not be culpable and deserving of the punishment usually indicated. Instead, 'treatment' for the 'illness' will be indicated. In law to commit a criminal offence one needs: *actus reus* (the act) and *mens rea* (intention).

The companion volume to this text, *The AMHP's Guide to Mental Health Law* (Brown, 2009), contains a flowchart and analysis of the major pieces of relevant law; this guide confines itself to a practical summary of where psychiatrists become involved.

Psychiatric reports

The main job of the psychiatrist is to detect whether a mental disorder is present and advise on its effect on *mens rea*. Psychiatric reports may be requested by defence solicitors, the court, the prison system or the Crown Prosecution Service.

After conviction

Psychiatric reports may be requested by the Magistrates' court after conviction, particularly of minor offences, where the psychiatric evidence will be taken in mitigation. That is to say, psychiatric evidence will be used to mitigate the harshness of the sentence or may be used to support an alternative to custody like a probation order or hospital treatment. Magistrates' courts often look for alternatives to custody and the forensic psychiatrist's job will be to give the magistrate some understanding of the offence in relation to the client's problem.

Before conviction, i.e. information relating to the verdict

In these cases the psychiatrist will be called upon to examine the client, produce reports and sometimes appear in court to support a number of psychiatric defences. These are:

- not guilty by reason of insanity;
- diminished responsibility;
- automatism;
- infanticide;
- unfitness to plead.

Psychiatric defences

Not guilty by reason of insanity

It is accepted the offence was committed but the defence suggests the client should be acquitted because their *mens rea* was 'insane'.

This defence can be raised for any offence, form shoplifting to murder.

The legal definition of insanity is the McNaghten rules: the defence must show that at the time of the offence the defendant was suffering from a disease of the mind which meant that either:

1. he or she did not know what they were doing; or

2. if they did they did not know it was wrong.

(Note the heavy emphasis on knowledge and reason; there is no mention of mood state or situation.)

If the insanity defence is successful the defendant is acquitted but there is an automatic disposal to hospital (generally secure but doesn't have to be) under a restriction order (i.e. at the discretion of the Home Office and Home Secretary). This defence was mainly used when we had capital punishment and is now rarely used except for serious murders.

Diminished responsibility

This is only used in murder cases. It is raised by the defence in which it is stated the defendant will plead not guilty to murder but guilty to manslaughter on the grounds of diminished responsibility. This avoids the mandatory life sentence for murder and allows the judge wide discretion in sentencing. The defence must show that at the time of the offence, the defendant was suffering from an 'abnormality of mind' that 'substantially impaired his or her responsibilities'. If both prosecution and defence agree, then there is usually only a brief trial and a psychiatric disposal. It is still possible to give a life sentence even though the diminished plea is accepted. The chief problem with this defence is that responsibility is not an easily measurable quality like a hormone but rather lies on a continuum and is affected by neurological, psychological and social factors.

Automatism

When this defence is raised the defence suggests at the time of the offence the defendant had no *mens rea* at all. The defence can raise the issue of automatism, but this may be problematic because the prosecution will usually counter by suggesting that the defendant is legally insane (see above). The defence will try and produce evidence to suggest the automatism is a sane one, and the prosecution will produce evidence to suggest it is an insane one. The judge will decide and instruct the jury. Sane automatism will bring about acquittal of the defendant. Insane automatism brings about an insanity verdict. Increasingly these defences have been restricted by the courts and they are not that often used.

Infanticide

If a mother kills her child while that child is under a year old then she may plead not guilty to murder but guilty of infanticide and receive the same penalties as a manslaughter verdict. This is a rather elderly piece of legislation and arises from the belief that the effects of lactation were deleterious to a woman's mind; more pertinently, perhaps, it is used in cases of post-natal depression.

Unfitness to plead

In order for a trial to start, the accused must be fit to plead. This means that the accused must be able to distinguish between a plea of guilty and not guilty, instruct counsel, challenge juries and follow the course of the trial. If the accused is found not fit to plead then under the terms of the Criminal Procedures (Insanity) Act 1964, as amended in 1991, they can be detained in a psychiatric hospital at the Home Office's discretion until fit to plead (i.e. just like an insanity verdict). In theory the accused could then return to court when fit to plead but in practice there are practical problems about reopening cases and many such patients languish for a long time in psychiatric hospitals under restriction orders when they have not yet been proven guilty. Accordingly, patients are not often found unfit to plead but are usually remanded to hospital for treatment under a section of the Mental Health Act. They can then be returned to court when they are better.

Psychiatric disposals under the Mental Health Act 1983

(See Table 6.1 for a summary of the relevant sections. For more detailed information see the companion text, *The AMHP's; Guide to Mental Health Law*.)

Table 6.1 Periods of detention, consent to treatment and access to MHTs for patients covered by Part III of the Mental Health Act 1983

Section number and purpose	Maximum duration	Can patient apply to MHT?	Can nearest relative apply to MHT?	Will there be an automatic MHT hearing?	Do consent to treatment rules apply?[1]
35 Remand to hospital for psychiatric report	**28 days** May be renewed by court for further 28 days to max. 12 weeks	No	There is no nearest relative	No	No
36 Remand to hospital for psychiatric treatment	**28 days** May be renewed by court for further 28 days to max. 12 weeks	No	There is no nearest relative	No	Yes
37 Guardianship order by court	**6 months** May be renewed for 6 months and then yearly	Within first 6 months and then in each period	Within first year and then yearly	No	No
37 Hospital order by court	**6 months** May be renewed for 6 months and then yearly	In second 6 months and then in each period	In second 6 months and then in each period	If one has not been held, the hospital managers refer to MHT every 3 years	Yes
37/41 Restriction order by court	**Variable**	In second 6 months and then yearly	There is no nearest relative	If one has not been held, Justice Secretary refers to MHT every 3 years	Yes
38 Interim hospital order by court	**12 weeks** May be renewed by 28 days at a time to max. 1 year	No	There is no nearest relative	No	Yes
45A Hospital and limited directions	**Without limit of time**	In first 6 months, second 6 months and then yearly	No	If one has not been held, the Justice Secretary refers to MHT every 3 years	Yes
47 Transfer to a hospital of a person serving prison sentence	**6 months** May be renewed for 6 months and then yearly	Within first 6 months and then in each period	No	If one has not been held, the hospital managers refer to MHT every 3 years	Yes
47/49 Transfer from prison plus restrictions	Restriction order expires on earliest prison release date.	In second 6-month period after transfer and then yearly	There is no nearest relative	If one has not been held, the Justice Secretary refers to MHT every 3 years	Yes
48 Transfer to hospital of other prisoners	**Variable**	Within first 6 months and then in each period	No	If one not has been held, the Justice Secretary refers to MHT every 3 years	Yes
48/49 Transfer from prison and restrictions	Restriction order expires on the earliest date of release from prison	In second 6-month period after transfer and then yearly	There is no nearest relative	If one has not been held, the Justice Secretary refers to MHT every 3 years	Yes
136 Police power in public places	**72 hours** Not renewable	No	No	No	No

1. Where consent to treatment rules do not apply, a patient is in the same position as an informal patient and should not be treated without their consent except for Mental Capacity Act treatment or in an emergency under common law.
   - Under section 67 the Secretary of State for Health can refer section 37 patients to the MHRT at any time.
   - Under section 71 the Home Secretary can refer restricted patients to the MHRT at any time.
   - Conditionally discharged restricted patients may apply to the MHRT after one year and then every two years but if the patient is recalled to hospital the Home Secretary must refer to the MHRT within one month.

Source: Brown (2009).

Section 35 is a remand section (i.e. unconvicted prisoner) from prison to hospital for assessment. It lasts for a maximum of 28 days in the first instance and can be renewed for further 28-day periods to a maximum of 12 weeks. Patients on section 35 are *not* covered by the consent to treatment provisions in Part IV of the Mental Health Act 1983.

Section 36 is another remand order which allows the treatment of the patient against their will while on remand from prison to hospital. This is important because patients cannot be treated against their will in prison except in an emergency. Patients on section 36 are covered by the consent to treatment provisions in Part IV of the Mental Health Act 1983.

Section 37 is the commonest hospital order which is generally applied to convicted prisoners in place of a prison sentence. It is essentially the same as section 3 of the Mental Health Act and it can be lifted any time by the responsible clinician (RC).

The Mental Health Tribunal (MHT) can discharge a patient from the section 37. Problems only arise when section 37 is combined with a section 41 which is known as a restriction order. This means that the patient's liberty is curtailed by the Ministry of Justice and that formal requests must be made to that office before the patient can be moved or discharged. Section 41 is applied by a judge, who has taken medical evidence, and is usually applied to patients thought to be particularly dangerous. The Mental Health Tribunal can discharge this group of patients but the RC and nearest relative cannot do so.

Section 38 is an interim hospital order (to assess suitability for section 37). It lasts for up to 12 weeks in the first instance and can be renewed by the court for up to a maximum of a year. It is often used as an assessment order to assess the appropriateness of treatment for personality disorder.

Section 45A was brought in by the Crime (Sentences) Act 1997. It is referred to as the 'hybrid order' as it is a prison sentence accompanied by hospital and limitation directions. It is only available to the Crown Court. Written or oral evidence from two doctors is required and the appropriate medical treatment test applies.

Section 47 allows for the transfer of convicted prisoners to psychiatric hospitals. Section 47 may be accompanied by a restriction direction so that the responsible clinician cannot allow the patient out of the hospital and leave must be applied for to do so to the Ministry.

Conditionally discharged patients under the Mental Health Act 1983

The notes for the Guidance of Social Supervisors, published by the Home Office, Department of Health and the Welsh Office in 1997 stated, that there were about 2,700 restricted patients detained in hospital. Sixty per cent have convictions for violence against the person, 12 per cent for sexual offences, 12 per cent for arson.

The number of conditionally discharged patients under active supervision in the community is estimated at 1,200. Supervisors are social service department staff or probation officers.

The purpose of social supervision is to protect the public from further serious harm by:

- assisting the patient's successful reintegration into the community;

- close monitoring of the patient's progress so that, in the event of subsequent deterioration of the patient's mental health or of a perceived increase in the risk of danger to the public, steps can be taken to assist the patient and protect the public.

It also allows for assessment in the community before granting an absolute discharge.

Ethical issues in forensic pyschiatry

A tension exists between the interests of the client and one's therapeutic duty towards them and one's duty to respect their autonomy and on the other hand one's duty to society. This tension, particularly in relation to society's interests, runs throughout forensic psychiatry and indeed with all those who work with offenders. This is obviously particularly highlighted in relation to childcare cases and a persistent anxiety is that forensic psychiatry may be used as an agent of social control and asked to comment on issues that it knows nothing about, e.g. 'fitness to parent'.

Forensic psychiatry can only comment on the presence or absence of mental illness which may or may not have anything to do with the rule-breaking behaviour which is being considered by the court. A forensic psychiatrist does not find out whether crimes have been committed, cannot establish whether a defendant is telling the truth and does not assess fitness to parent. If he or she sees patients solely for the purposes of third parties (such as the Crown or insurance defendants) then he or she advises the evaluee accordingly that they do not have to talk to her.

The main ethical issues for psychiatrists relate to the following:

- *Treatability*:

  - Are we treating the illness or the behaviour?

  - How do we know when someone is 'cured'?

- *Dangerousness*. The assessment of dangerousness is very much a gamble of a number of variables. The best predictor of future violence is past violence but several studies have shown that psychiatrists are no better than the general public at predicting who will be dangerous and that a prediction of personal violence such as homicide is as erratic as a prediction of suicide (i.e. there are some that you will never be able to foresee). Clearly also socio-cultural perception will enter into the assessment of dangerousness and prejudice is a danger. Once again this raises the question of whether the psychiatrist is acting as a public order service rather than a service for the mentally ill.

- *Confidentiality*. Information about the patient may belong to:
  - the patient;
  - the defence solicitor;
  - the court;
  - the hospital managers.

  At all times it is necessary to try and work out who will have access to the information and whose interests are one's first duty. Problems arise when the patient makes one aware that he or she is offending – there is no legal duty to do anything, but there may be an ethical duty to do so.

In summary the ethical questions may be analysed using these three questions:

1. To whom do you owe a duty?

2. What does that duty consist of?

3. What is the scope of that duty?

Chapter 7
Psychiatry of old age

As the population ages, so the need for psychiatric services for the elderly grows. In the past, an old-age psychiatrist worked principally with patients who had senile dementia and their families. Now old-age psychiatrists will be working with patients over 65 who have other problems apart from dementia: who suffer from anxiety disorders, depression, psychotic disorders and even substance misuse, especially alcohol.

Assessment and treatment of psychiatric conditions in older people is the same as for younger people. Essentially, the psychiatry of old age is the same as general psychiatry, with a particular population. Although it is true that a sub-group of older patients will suffer from age-specific disorders such as dementia, many more will suffer from a wide range of psychiatric disorders and psychological distress relating to their personal experience. There are many ways to be old in twenty-first century western cultures, and old-age psychiatric services need to address all of them.

Dementia and the ageing brain

Dementia is a progressive decline in mental functions due to organic brain disease. There are many different causes of dementia, and some of them are specifically associated with ageing.

Symptoms of dementia

The symptoms of dementia arise from the destruction of brain tissue, especially in the frontal lobes. These are the parts of the brain that support both personality and memory, hence these are the symptoms that affect personal identity and cause so much distress to relatives. Symptoms include a gradual decline in memory, especially for recent events, and conscious monitoring of current awareness so that patients do not retain new information. This leads to wandering, disorientation and confusion. As the disease gets worse and more brain tissue is lost, the patient loses the capacity for abstract thought, language deteriorates and earlier memories start to be affected.

Damage to the frontal lobes affects social behaviour and the observation of social rules, so there is social disinhibition, especially as patients may lose their normal emotional responses to social situations. This can result in unusual verbal and physical behaviours, urinary and bowel incontinence and inappropriate conversation. In the latter stages, recognition of important social figures such as family and friends is lost, and this loss of connection seems to result in loss of personal identity. Interestingly, this loss of personal identity is associated with decreased physical function and physical withdrawal; it usually heralds the beginning of physical decline which results in illnesses that may be fatal.

Types of dementia

- Alzheimer's disease is the most common type of dementia and approximately 1 per cent of the over 65s rising to 20 per cent of the over 80s have this type of dementia. In Alzheimer's disease, there is brain shrinkage and deposition of a substance called amyloid which damages brain cells. There is also evidence of damage to the acetylcholine regulation. There is some evidence that Alzheimer's runs in families and may be associated with vulnerability of the brain to aluminium. There is a lack of good quality evidence about the causes of these dementias.

- Pick's disease and Lewy body dementia are less common types of dementia that can affect the ageing brain. They also can affect those under 65.

- Chronic alcoholism can result in early dementia but may be reduced in its impact if the person can stop drinking. Also related to alcohol abuse is Korsakoff's dementia, which is caused by a lack of thiamine as a result of prolonged alcohol abuse. This dementia is potentially partially reversible, so it is important to exclude this in an older person with signs of dementia who also has a history of alcohol abuse.

- Repeated brain injuries or loss of blood flow (infarction) can result in a particular pattern of dementia. This is associated with chronic high blood pressure causing small bleeds into the brain. It may be possible to delay its progress if the hypertension is treated.

Treatment and management of dementia

In the last ten years, drugs have been developed that help delay the dementing process. These drugs do not cure dementia but can delay cognitive damage and may allow patients to remain independent for longer and for personal identity to be preserved. They are not always successful, however, and the effect is temporary at best.

There are considerable debates about the use of these drugs because of their limited benefit and their cost. However, most old-age psychiatrists do prescribe them.

Dementia patients may develop symptoms of depression, anxiety and psychotic symptoms as their disease advances. Relevant medications may be prescribed for these symptoms. However, all psychotropic drugs may cause confusion in the elderly, so they need to be prescribed with care.

Finally, it is well known that carers and supporters of those with dementia need psychological support and advice. Old-age psychiatrists can assist by liaising with voluntary sector and community networks.

Depression in old age

A definition of depression

> *Prolonged sad mood (more than two weeks) with accompanying biological features, which is sufficiently severe and prolonged as to impair quality of life.*

Prevalence

Probably somewhere between 13 and 17 per cent of people over 65 suffer depression. Women over the age of 65 have decreased neurotransmitter levels and so have a natural tendency to depression. Depression is often present but not diagnosed in older patients, which is particularly unfortunate as 60–80 per cent of people respond well to treatment.

Aetiology

The causes of depression in old age are similar to those in younger people. There are individuals who are more at risk of depression generally, such as those with a strong family history, a history of depression and a history of childhood trauma. However, individuals with these risk factors may become depressed for the first time in older age because of exposure to loss events. It is well known that loss events can precipitate depression, and older people are exposed to more loss events than most.

Loss events that particularly affect the elderly are loss of occupation, loss of bodily integrity and loss of friends. Our jobs, our health and our friends are important constituents of our personal and social identity, and if these are damaged or lost, then this represents a major stressor for human beings. The loss of employment, or specifically occupation, may mean a major loss of identity for some individuals, perhaps especially for men for whom masculine gender role identity may be more strongly linked with work than friends or family. Retirement obviously can have a real impact on income and life style as well as the loss of a social circle.

Retirement is one cause of loss of friends, but in older age, friends start to be lost through death or illness. Individuals who have a wide social circle may lose this if they become ill and have to move house to be near potential carers. Friends themselves grow old and die; it is not uncommon for people in their 80s to find that all their friends who knew them as young people have died so that they feel abandoned and bereft. Partners also may die causing disruption of long attachments, and as one gets older, it is more likely that one will be affected by the experience of sudden traumatic losses of younger people through rare diseases or accidents.

Finally, the loss of youth and good health is a potent risk factor for depression. Feeling unwell or in pain lowers the mood and arousal levels, and any chronic illness associated with the ageing process (such as osteoarthritis or back problems) can cause depression. There is also the issue (in western societies at least) of the loss of good looks and sexual attractiveness – a further loss of a type of identity that brought pleasure.

All these loss events go to affect the experience of the older person and increase their risk of becoming depressed. The ubiquity of these factors may explain why men and women are more equally affected by depression in old age than when younger.

The symptoms of depression

In the elderly these are the same as in younger people. However, in the elderly, depression can present principally as irritability, and also as mild confusion and cognitive decline and with more emphasis on physical (somatic) complaints. Sleep and appetite disturbance should be enquired for, and older age should not mean that sexual function is not also an issue. As for younger people, a sub-group of patients may develop a severe depression with psychotic features which carries a high risk of morbidity.

Assessment and treatment

The Geriatric Depression Scale (15-item version)
This is a useful screening tool for depression in older patients.

Are you basically satisfied with your life?	Yes/**NO**
Have you dropped many of your activities and interests?	**YES**/No
Do you feel that your life is empty?	**YES**/No
Do you often get bored?	**YES**/No
Are you in good spirits most of the time?	Yes/**NO**
Are you afraid that something bad is going to happen to you?	**YES**/No
Do you feel happy most of the time?	Yes/**NO**
Do you often feel helpless?	**YES**/No
Do you prefer to stay at home, rather than going out and doing new things?	**YES**/No
Do you feel that you have more problems with memory than most?	**YES**/No
Do you think it is wonderful to be alive now?	Yes/**NO**
Do you feel pretty worthless the way you are now?	**YES**/No
Do you feel full of energy?	Yes/**NO**
Do you feel that your situation is hopeless?	**YES**/No
Do you feel that most people are better off than you are?	**YES**/No

Score 1 for answers in **capitals**: 0–5 not depressed; 6–15 depressed.

It is essential to conduct a full assessment to clearly identify the problem and there should be reassessment at regular intervals. There is a real risk of failing to do this with older patients. Treatments include medication and psychological therapies as appropriate. One caveat is that older people may have less good kidney and liver function, so that drug dosages may have to be adjusted down.

It is easy for elderly people to be made more confused by their medication, because the dose is too great for them or because their psychiatric medications have an effect on some other physical condition. The ageing brain is particularly susceptible to drugs that alter consciousness/awareness such as sedatives and sleeping tablets, so these need to be given cautiously and with monitoring.

Because many older people do have some degree of physical problems that make medication complicated, it is important to consider non-pharmacological types of interventions, such as psychological therapies and social supports and contact. In relation to severe depression, ECT may be the treatment of choice, because it is quicker in effect than waiting for anti-depressant medication to fully work.

All the psychological therapies may be helpful in older patients, depending on their individual profile. Dementing patients may not be able to use cognitive interventions but may benefit from structured group therapies that allow them to connect to others. If there are no concerns about cognitive decline, then all the psychological therapies may be effective and can be offered to patients.

Other psychiatric disorders of old age

It is rare for an individual to develop a severe mental illness in the sixth and seventh decade if they have not previously had such an illness. However, it does occur occasionally and patients may present with new affective disorders or paraphrenia (schizophrenia in older age). Other causes of brain disease should be excluded, especially brain tumours, secondary tumours from another primary cancer site and early dementia.

It is important to remember that the elderly may abuse drugs, both legal and illegal, and that they may act violently when mentally ill, like any other patient. The risk is small but present for the elderly in the same ways. Similarly the risk of suicide is present, and may be increased in older male patients, especially those with a history of substance misuse.

Chapter 8

Psychiatry and risk assessment

Conducting a full assessment of risk

Risk assessment is not about 100 per cent accurate predictions or the avoidance of all risk. Rather it is about making a clinical, logical, medico-legally defensible decision.

The Kim Kirkman Inquiry Panel concluded that the following all played a part in making a decision about risk:

- the past history of the patient;
- self-reporting by the patient at interview;
- observation of the behaviour and mental state of the patient;
- discrepancies between what is reported and what is observed;
- psychological* and, if appropriate, physiological tests;
- statistics derived from studies of related cases;
- prediction indicators derived from research.

[* By a chartered psychologist or under the supervision of one. (West Midlands Regional Health Authority, 1991)]

In the panel's words:

> The decision on risk is made when all these strands come together in what is known as 'clinical judgement', a balanced summary of prediction derived from knowledge of the individual, the present circumstances and what is known about the disorder from which he [or she] suffers.

Note that the most significant predictors of violence are (in order):

- being male;
- aged 18–29;
- of a lower socio-economic group;
- socially isolated and alone (especially separated or divorced);

- engaged in substance abuse (or dual diagnosis);
- history of arrest (or arrest and detention);
- presence of ASPD.

Key elements in the assessment of risk

A risk assessment needs to consider all the possible risk factors, look at the social context of the individual, look at different aspects of the individual's history and consider changes over time.

Questions to consider include the following:

- Is there any risk of harm?
- If so, what sort of harm and of what likely degree (nature and magnitude)?
- How likely is it that harm will actually occur?
- What is its immediacy or imminence?
- How long will the risk last?
- What factors contribute to the risk?
- How can the factors be modified or managed?

The bare *minimum* for a risk assessment of a patient is to:

- ask the patient for any history of violence;
- ask the patient for current thoughts of violence;
- attempt to contact an informant and ask about any violence from the patient;
- request previous discharge summaries;
- document the above and the outcome.

Individual risk assessment includes the following:

- What are the demographic characteristics?
- What is the history of violent behaviour?
- What is the base rate of violent behaviour in people with the same background?
- What are the sources of stress in the person's current environment?
- What are the cognitive and emotional factors which increase violent behaviour?
- What are the cognitive and emotional factors which decrease violent behaviour?
- Are there similarities of context with past violence and likely future contexts?
- Who are the likely victims and how available are they?
- What means does the person possess?

Categories of seriousness in risk assessment

Level 1: More serious

- Used weapon
- Threatened with weapon in hand
- Sexual assault
- Any other violence with injury (includes bruises, cuts, broken bones/teeth, stab, gunshot, death).

Level 2: Less serious

- Threw object
- Pushed, grabbed, shoved
- Slapped (no injury)
- Kicked, bit, choked
- Hit with fist or object.

Neither level includes spanking, violence in self-defence or institutional violence.

Mental state examination

(See also Chapter 2.)

Items to consider include:

- *Subjective feelings of tension or explosiveness* – ideas or feelings of violence.
- *Persecutory ideas* – feelings of fear, especially delusions: intensity and preoccupation, who is being incorporated into the delusional system?
- *Passivity phenomena* – important association of 'threat/control-override'; symptoms with violence.
- *Hallucinations* – nature and quality; whether source is benevolent or malevolent, plus omnipotence of source (what are the consequences of not complying with any commands, why comply with some and not others?).
- *Depression* – feelings of hopelessness, e.g. 'I wish I was dead – there's nothing to live for – I might as well kill her and the children too – I don't care anymore'.
- *Jealousy of morbid intensity* – nature and detail.
- *Insight* – not only of psychiatric disorder but into previous violent/aggressive behaviour.

Management of risk

It is advisable to consult with others and then to consider the following for high-risk patients:

- detention under the Mental Health Act 1983;
- 'target hardening' (warning the potential victim);
- intensified treatment (increased frequency of sessions, increased medication, joint sessions with others);
- supervised aftercare;
- involvement of the police.

Measures should be specific, proportionate and rational.

Statistics on homicides and mental disorder

Of 500 homicide convictions in England and Wales each year:

- 400 are seen as normal legally;
- 100 seen as abnormal.

Of this 100, in any year:

- infanticide would account for 1–10;
- insanity/unfitness to plead would account for 1–5;
- manslaughter/diminished responsibility would account for 70–80 (half of these transferred to hospital).

Note: In 35–50 cases of homicide each year the perpetrator commits suicide.

Issues concerning personality disorder and violence

(See also Chapter 5.)

Features identified in DSM III-R are: anti-social borderline, histrionic, narcissistic.

ICD10 identifies: dis-social, emotionally unstable, impulsive, borderline type and histrionic behaviours.

Hare (1991) described two sets of personality traits that relate to severe criminality and cruelty:

- Factor 1: glibness, lack of remorse, callousness, lack of empathy, irresponsibility.
- Factor 2: criminality, history of conduct disorder, cruelty, general social deviance.

Some implications of psychopathic individuals are as follows:

- deviates from forensic 'norm';

- limited place for drug treatment;
- increased need for psychological services;
- problems of sympathy and empathy;
- likelihood of child abuse history.

Special problems arise when there is an overlap of mental illness, personality disorder and substance abuse (the 'triple whammy').

Treatability will link to the following factors:

- the patient and their history;
- the nature of the disorder;
- the doctors and their institution;
- scientific knowledge;
- duration and history of the disorder;
- resources.

Chapter 9
Patients as parents

Like many other medical specialities, psychiatry has traditionally considered the patient as an independent unit and not thought about the implications of ill health on the family as a whole. In this section, we discuss psychiatric patients who are parents and the implications for their children, especially in terms of risk, and advice for family courts who have to consider the welfare of children.

Frequency and general issues

Prevalence

Given the high prevalence of various types of mental disorder in the community, it is not surprising that a substantial population of psychiatric service users have children for whom they are responsible. Sixty per cent of the seriously mentally ill patients living in the community have children under 16; 25 per cent have children under the age of five. This means that the majority of the caseload of a community mental health team (CMHT) will involve relating to children and young adults who may need help and support in relation to their mentally ill parent.

There is a particular issue for services for women with post-natal disorders, who by definition will be vulnerable patients with highly vulnerable children. Twenty-five per cent of women referred to psychiatric services have children under five, and it is likely that they have been referred because of concerns about how they are coping with the youngest child. Depression in women is associated with having three children under the age of ten and a lack of a supportive relationship, because care of small children is psychologically stressful, especially in those women who are psychiatrically vulnerable because they had poor parenting themselves.

Assessing if a child's needs are being met

When a parent has a psychiatric illness how much does the parent's problems interfere with parenting skills and lead to possible harm in the child? This is a question that all professionals need to ask when working with a patient who is a parent. The focus needs to be on the child's needs and seeing the situation from the child's view.

Possible risks to children from parents with mental disorders

Children are most at risk of abuse, cruelty and death at the hands of their parents, regardless of the presence or absence of mental disorder. Each year in England and Wales, 100 children are killed, and 80 of those will be killed by their parents. A study of child homicides showed that approximately 30 per cent of those parents suffered from a mental disorder – a higher than usual proportion compared to the general population, but a minority in terms of those who kill children. Of those parents, the majority were women suffering from some form of post-natal illness; however, it is possible that the figures may have been based on psychiatric evidence given at trial rather than actual psychiatric histories.

The point here is that most mentally ill parents will not pose a direct risk to their children in terms of violent assault. Just as for adults, there are mental disorders in parents which are associated with increased risk of violence to children – chiefly paranoid psychoses (which are common post-natally in women) and ASPD.

With respect to child abuse, studies of maltreating parents have showed higher than usual prevalence of personality disorder, usually ASPD (in fathers) and BPD (in mothers). But this is not say that child maltreatment is caused by the presence of a personality disorder alone. Child maltreatment is usually the result of multiple risk factors operating simultaneously, and the fact that a parent has a personality disorder does not predict future abuse.

Again, in relation to child abuse, it is well established that a significant proportion of abusers have themselves been abused as children. However, this does not allow us to view adults who have been abused as being at increased risk of abusing their children, because retrospective data analysis does not allow prospective prediction. In fact, there is some evidence to suggest that adults who were abused as children take active steps to protect their children, and therefore may be at less risk of future abuse overall.

What these facts should make clear is that risk assessment in any parent is complex, and even more so for parents with mental disorders. The biggest problem faced by children whose parents have mental illnesses is that these parents are unlikely to be able to soothe and calm their children's fears, and may even be a source of fear to their children, without intending to be so. A mother who is intermittently psychotic may never harm her child physically, but witnessing her disordered mental states may be extremely frightening for that child. Chronic and repeated fear states are bad for children's psychological development; they interfere with attachment behaviours and, cognitive development, especially memory systems and affect regulation. Sadly, it is this problem that is the key issue for parents with psychiatric disorders, and it may be one that they have little conscious control over.

The specific problems of different disorders in terms of parenting are described below.

Psychiatric diagnoses and the effect of these on the ability to parent

Depression

This area has been most widely researched but has usually looked at depressed mothers rather than depressed parents. Depression can lead to irritability, insensitivity and unavailability of maternal support. Depressed mothers may feel hostile towards their children, or may provoke anger and distress in the infant, but be unable to soothe the child. This can disrupt the infant's ability to modulate affect and arousal. Depressed mothers can also find managing distress in their infants very difficult. This can lead to insecure attachment in the infant. Normally secure attachment depends on many factors such as availability, sensitivity and responding to baby's distress, and these can all be quite difficult for a depressed mother. Also the development of self-esteem in the child can be damaged by an over-critical mother. The ability to establish relationships is also formed in these early years and potentially can be diminished if the mother is depressed. Finally there is good evidence that even moderate degrees of depression in mothers can lead to reduced cognitive development in their children.

Post-natal depression

Lynne Murray (Murray and Cooper, 1999) and others have done extensive work looking at the normal communication between very young babies and their mother. Facial expressions and vocal noises form early 'conversations' from birth (and in pre-term babies). This early communication facilitates normal emotional development and cognitive skills. It is thought that post-natal depression can interfere with this. IQ drop, behavioural disturbance at school and emotional disturbance are seen, particularly in boys of post-natally depressed mothers.

Psychotic disorders

Parents with chronic psychotic disorders (such as schizophrenia) typically suffer from negative symptoms which mimic depression and therefore the problems seen with depression can be seen with chronic psychosis. Parents may seem particularly withdrawn and detachment is a problem. The patient can be absorbed in their inner world and not be available to the child. The effects of medication, which can be sedating, may also cause the parent to be unavailable or unintentionally neglectful.

Acute psychosis

Unpredictable, chaotic, acute psychotic breakdowns in parents can be very harmful, partly because they are frightening for the child, and partly because a psychotic parent may pose a very real risk to the child's care. Lack of insight into illness and lack of insight into the child's needs may be seen with acute psychosis, also causing a risk to child safety. However, parental care may be good enough between episodes.

The child is particularly at risk if they are involved in the parent's delusional system. However, this is fortunately very rare. Obviously if these delusions are acted upon (e.g. a child is raised as the opposite sex because of a delusional belief), this can be very harmful to the child. Any delusional system involving another human being is potentially risky, and if it involves children, then they are that much more at risk because of their vulnerability and dependence.

Post-natal (puerperal) psychosis

This is the most well known and most risky form of acute psychosis and is found in 1 in 500 mothers. Mothers with this type of acute psychosis have highly changeable mental states and can easily appear to be quite well for the duration of a mental state assessment.

Mothers with paranoid psychoses may be especially careful to hide their symptoms. It is therefore essential to carry out repeat assessments, and involve as many staff as possible to monitor and support the family. Mothers with post-natal psychosis should be admitted to hospital and treated as soon as possible, because these conditions respond well to treatment and are often short-lived (1–2 weeks). They will remit spontaneously and in theory mothers could be managed in the community, but the established risk to new babies is so well known that it is negligent not to admit – using the powers of the Mental Health Act if necessary. Full recovery is nearly always seen and the relationship between the mother and the baby is usually good. Such mothers need support and reassurance afterwards, not least because they are at increased risk of becoming psychotic again if they have another child. Their risk of psychotic breakdown generally seems to be increased also.

Anxiety disorders

Maternal anxiety can lead to poor child adjustment and behaviour problems because the mother is unavailable or often in conflict with the child. There is an association seen between school refusal and agoraphobia. Phobic conditions can lead to avoidance of the feared object and can impact on childcare. Obsessive compulsive disorder (OCD) rituals can often involve the child. The child can be vigorously cleaned so that their skin can be raw and broken. Also a child can be involved in actually carrying out the rituals such as repeated checking of switches or locks with obvious distress to the child. Rituals can be very time-consuming and divert energy away from childcare so that the child's needs are neglected.

Eating disorders

Bulimia and anorexia nervosa are often very concealed and their impact on childcare is difficult to assess. Research has shown that there is often difficulty with feeding babies and small children, leading to failure to thrive. Mothers with eating disorders can be over-concerned with the child's body weight and shape and severe dietary regimes are sometimes seen, as well as more covert conflict. In bulimia mothers can ignore or even punish the child during binges.

Somatising disorder

Children of somatising parents are often presented to doctors as ill, and later become anxious children who have somatising disorders themselves. It is possible that some somatising parents may be at risk of making their children ill deliberately (what has been called 'Münchausen's syndrome by proxy' or paediatric factitious disorder).

Deliberate self-harm

Deliberate self-harm (DSH) is often a behavioural expression of distress in the parent and is associated with difficulties in expressing rage, hostility and grief. Parents who cannot manage their own negative affects are unlikely to be able to manage their children's, and they may respond to their child's distress with fear or violence. There is some evidence to suggest that a self-harming parent is at increased risk of child maltreatment. It should also be remembered that the experience of seeing a parent hurt themselves is distressing and frightening for children, and this alone is bad for their development. When assessing a patient who has self-harmed, their parental status should be asked for and the childcare perspective needs to be considered. In rare cases the child can be directly involved leading to injuries and fatalities.

Alcohol and drug abuse

In all cases of alcohol and drug abuse, childcare can be affected by the following factors:

- diversion of resources away from childcare to resourcing the addiction;
- criminal activity to fund the addiction;
- exposure to violence;
- changeable mental state;
- stigma and shame for child, particularly school-age children;
- an intoxicated parent may not be able to provide a safe home environment, so safety issues are important and accidents are seen;
- an addicted parent can fail to prioritise the children's needs above their own addiction;
- the child can be become the inappropriate carer of the intoxicated parent or parent in withdrawal.

Alcohol and other depressants can lead to problems of disinhibition and violence. With intoxication, sedation, coma and fitting can occur. With habituation come withdrawal symptoms. Long-term physical and cognitive impairment can also be a problem. With opiates there are problems of withdrawal and unavailability of parent when intoxicated. With habituation come the symptoms of withdrawal, which can impact upon a child, e.g. irritability. Stimulant drugs such as amphetamines and cocaine can lead to psychosis and chronic depression. The impact of this on childcare is discussed above. Hallucinogenic drugs can lead to psychosis-like states and the problem of parents being in charge of a child when out of touch with reality.

Perinatal problems with alcohol and drugs

Much is known about the foetal alcohol syndrome which is the condition seen in extreme alcohol abuse in pregnancy. More mild problems are seen with lesser degrees of alcohol abuse such as small babies. Chaotic drug misuse can lead to low birth weight babies, toxaemia, bleeding in pregnancy, foetal distress and even malformations. Withdrawal from opiates after birth leads to jittery babies, poor feeding and fitting. Withdrawal from diazepam during pregnancy can lead to fitting and miscarriage or stillbirth.

Prescribed drugs in pregnancy

It is now well recognised that mental illness has toxic effects on an unborn baby. Abrupt withdrawal of medication at any time is not wise as this can lead to an increased rate of relapse. This is particularly the case during pregnancy. Therefore pregnancy in a woman known to be suffering from mental illness or have a history of mental illness needs to be very cautiously dealt with. Referral to a psychiatrist is advised.

Because new medicines cannot be tested in pregnancy it takes time to build up safety information. For this reason it is often the case that more is known about outcomes in pregnancy with older drugs. Absolute safety information is rarely available but the British National Formulary (BNF) gives more specific advice for drugs while the National Teratology Information Service (NTIS – tel. 0191 232 1525) can give more specific advice for individual circumstances. In principle pregnancy should not be seen as an automatic stop on medication as the risks to the foetus of a relapsing condition may outweigh the risks associated with continued use of the drug.

With a planned pregnancy there should be time to identify an effective and low-risk treatment and a time when psychosocial stress factors are likely to be minimal

Child abuse and homicide

As described above, most parents who abuse or kill their children do not have established mental disorders. There are thought to be similarities between abusing mothers and depressed mothers. There is an association between the two as there are similar factors in both groups of mothers. Also depression can follow on after abuse. The common factors are inconsistency, hostility, provoking anxiety in the child and guilt-induced means of child rearing. Also physical care can be compromised. Failure to thrive in infants is seen in families where the mother is depressed. The mother can feel hopeless and lack energy. A mother's own self-care and appetite can be reduced and therefore she may forget to feed the child. Irritability can lead to conflict over feeding. Also traumas in the mother's own childhood can be reawakened in the relationship she has with her own children. Selma Fraiberg et al. have written extensively on this theme in *Ghosts in the nursery* (1980).

Infanticide

This is defined as the killing of a baby under one year old. The under-ones are four times more likely to be killed than any other age group in the general population, and 11–25 per cent of all homicide victims are children. Mentally ill parents, often the mother, usually carry out the killing. One or two children under the age of 16 are killed each week. There are between thirty and forty infanticide convictions per year (Infanticide Act 1938). This is considerable under-reporting as some babies are killed soon after delivery and never recorded as killings. With regard to reported cot deaths between 2 and 10 per cent may not actually be such. It is also important to recognise infanticide as an indicator of more widespread abuse. Infanticide is often the last act in a history of chronic and repeated physical abuse of a child.

The effect of age is quite marked. The risk of being killed falls off with each passing month. Male babies are more at risk but it is not clear why this should be the case. Mothers again are more likely to be the killer. If men kill they tend to use more violent methods and are then more likely to be imprisoned. Mothers smother and asphyxiate; men shake, batter or even shoot babies. As was noted in Chapter 6, if a mother kills her child while that child is under a year old then she may plead not guilty to murder but guilty of infanticide, and receive the same penalties as for a manslaughter verdict. This can be seen as the medicalisation of infanticide as it arises from the belief that the effects of lactation are deleterious to a woman's mind. It is sometimes used as a plea in cases of post-natal depression.

Other factors may be important such as social or economic problems, violence, poor relationships, personality dysfunction, fear of intimacy and dependency. In the D'Orban study (1979) the commonest form of killing in socio-economically deprived families was battering. D'Orban argued that socio-economic factors and violence were more important than psychiatric illness. However, it is notable that while social factors have changed historically the rate of infanticide has remained constant. Liberalisation of abortion has not affected infanticide rates. Homicide rates have increased but again there has been no change in infanticide rates.

The rate of infanticide is the same in both Scotland and England, whereas both homicide statistics and social factors vary considerably between the two countries. It may be that mental illness is the more consistent and important factor in infanticide. Certainly mental illness seems to be more likely to be a factor in the deaths of older children. However, in the various studies the rates of psychiatric illness vary between 27 and 90 per cent. Many of the studies have had quite widely varying methods of recording mental illness and the better and more recent studies suggest that between 30 and 40 per cent of all child deaths involve a mentally ill parent. Craig (2004) provides a good summary of the various research studies in this field.

Neonaticide

Neonaticide is defined as death within the first 24 hours. Between 20 and 25 per cent of infanticide is neonaticide so a child's first day carries the highest risk of being killed. It affects both sexes equally in terms of the child but the killer is usually the mother. In these cases there has often been denial of pregnancy. The mother can often be young and alone. Cases of disposal of unwanted children can lead to neonaticide. Early research concluded that most neonaticides were indeed the disposal of unwanted children (Resnick, 1970). However, more recent work has shown that neonaticide is often the act of very severely disturbed young women or girls with either psychiatric illness or personality disorders. These cases tend to be dealt with leniently in the courts in the UK even in the absence of mental illness.

A Study of Working Together – Part 8 Reports

This important study by Adrian Falkov (1995) relates to the deaths of under 16s thought to be due to abuse or killing. There are 120 per year on average. Falkov studied 100 of these. Thirty-two had positive psychiatric history in one of the parents. Of the remainder many had no clear indication either way. Of these 32 mentally ill cases 25 were perpetrators (19 women, 6 men) and 10 were partners (8 women and 2 men). The majority of mentally ill women were either perpetrators or, if partners, they had the main or sole childcare responsibilities. The study showed a cluster of maternal mental illness, childcare burden and perpetration. When these women are the mentally ill partners of perpetrators they are often younger than the partner, and there were frequently unplanned pregnancies and violent relationships. One explanation of the violence might be the threat to the parental relationship from the demands of the child. There was some evidence of a failure of mentally ill women to protect their children. Many such women may have insight and ask for help. Professionals involved can have a strong desire to support such young vulnerable woman especially when they are seen to be insightful in asking for help. However, the needs of the child for protection should be paramount.

There were the same number of males and females in this study. Of the children 79 per cent were under five; older deaths were more likely to be by non-psychiatrically ill perpetrators. About 80 per cent of the cases had recorded child protection concerns before the child's death. Two-thirds had child protection case conferences (CPCCs). In only a few cases did CPCCs involve adult mental health professionals. A higher proportion of non-psychiatric cases were accommodated than psychiatric cases.

In 27 per cent of the cases studied there were concerns for and even examples of the killing of other children. Therefore the focus needs to be on all of the children in the home and not just on one.

Mentally ill perpetrators were older than others and were more likely to be natural parents. There was relationship discord in about 70 per cent of the cases. Retaliatory killing (i.e. taking out anger with a partner on the child or getting revenge) was a frequent feature of the cases. Poor antenatal care, unplanned pregnancy and requests for adoption were all commonly seen. Methods used for killing were asphyxiation, use of implements or drowning. Non-mentally ill perpetrators more commonly used head injury to kill.

Half of those studied had a history of deliberate self-harm. Completed suicide after child killing is rare in the United Kingdom but commoner in other societies, e.g. 70 per cent of child killings in Sweden are followed by suicide.

Psychosis was the commonest diagnosis in both perpetrator and partner. There were also examples of depression, Münchausen by proxy and personality disorder.

In all of the Falkov cases many different agencies were involved. In one CPCC 80 professionals were invited. Forty per cent of mentally ill perpetrators had contact with psychiatric services in the month before death. A whole variety of different treatments in different settings were mentioned. Poor compliance with treatment was a common feature. In two cases an adult psychiatrist expressed grave concerns over risk to the children and these went unheeded. In eight cases information was withheld because of confidentiality. In the vast majority of cases there were no adult mental health representatives at CPCCs and there was a very marked lack of communication between all of these different agencies. The emphasis seems always to be on the wellness of the parent and a sense of false optimism. A focus on the needs of the ill parent seems to have occurred in some cases. The child is less likely to be taken into care if a parent is mentally ill.

Falkov concluded that reliance on traditional indices of risk should be considered: violence, isolation, discord, poor education and poor work record. He also concluded that there was a need for adult mental health professionals to communicate with other agencies and vice versa.

Factors to be considered when conducting an assessment of a patient as a parent

Factors relating to the illness

1. Is this an acute illness? What is the prognosis and time-scale for improvement? A lot can be tolerated in the short term that would not be deemed to be acceptable risk in the long term.

2. Different symptoms have different impact on a child. Research has shown that despair and misery are less damaging than hostility and irritability directed at a child.

3. Aggression, either verbal or physical, directed at a child is known to be damaging to a child and can lead to psychiatric problems.

4. A child who witnesses aggressive acts carried out on others is likely to be harmed in the long term.

Historical factors

1. Are significant others able to cope for the child in place of the family?

2. What is the child's previous experience of separation from the parents?

Factors relating to the parent

1. What is the insight of the parents into the child's needs?

2. What is the ability of the parent to prioritise a child's needs above its own even when mentally ill?

3. What is the insight of the parent into their illness?

4. Are the parents able to control their abnormal behaviour in front of the child for short periods of time and therefore protect the child from some aspects of their illness?

5. How co-operative is the parent with agencies such as mental health services and social services?

6. Is there coexisting dual diagnosis in the parent? Serious mental illness combined with either personality disorder or drug and alcohol abuse can lead to poor prognosis and poor functioning of the individual as a parent.

Factors relating to the child

1. What is the child's age? The child has different vulnerabilities at different stages, e.g. the infancy period is crucial in forming emotional stability for the child. Ages between 1 and 3 are crucial for development of secure attachment. During adolescence problems of separation and individuation and autonomy can be difficult, especially with a depressed parent.

2. What is the child's temperament? Is the child seen as being a difficult child or an irritable baby?

3. Does the child have a physical illness? Either illness or handicap can be an added stress to the family.

4. Does the child have a role as a carer? The child may be inappropriately used as carer of the mentally ill parent.

Social factors

1. Are there coexisting problems such as racial or ethnic isolation, socio-economic problems or family dysfunction? All these other problems combined with mental illness may mean that the family has less ability to cope with the parent's mental illness.

2. Does the child with a mentally ill parent suffer from social stigma and isolation? What is the impact of this on the child, particularly when of school age?

The assessment process

Dual parallel legislation exists in the form of the Mental Health Act 1983 and the Children Act 1989. The Mental Health Act is concerned with psychiatric diagnosis and adult civil rights. The Children Act is concerned with balancing the need of the child and the parents' responsibilities. The Mental Health Act alone will not protect the child.

Principle of paramountcy of children's interest – professional dilemmas

- Adult mental health teams may feel unable to express an opinion about separating a child from the parent as this might jeopardise the relationship they have with the patient. Separation from the child can be severely traumatising for the patient parent (and to adult mental health workers) but sometimes adult mental health workers are involved in making this decision. It is difficult to be seen as a caring professional while at the same time inflicting damage on the patient. A traumatised patient may end up trusting no one and therefore try to have a professional with the primary responsibility to the parent outside the child protection process. Nevertheless, all professionals need to recognise the child welfare issues and prioritise these.

- Adult mental health teams should focus on the therapeutic usefulness to the patient of being a parent. They may see childcare as a form of occupational therapy. This can ignore the needs of the child.

- Permission to break the confidentiality rule is clearly given in the addendum to the Children Act: 'Child protection: medical responsibilities'.

- All caring professionals should try to see the good aspects of how their patients function. It is sometimes difficult not to emphasise the positive points and to be critical. Criticising a patient's ability to function as a parent can feel like a fundamental criticism of her or him as a person.

The role of adult mental health workers

The role of the adult mental health worker is to:

- provide information about diagnosis, treatment and prognosis;

- provide information on the resources and limitations of mental health services – what can and can't be done;

- provide information on the effect of illness and medication on the parent's general functioning, relationship with the child and ability to parent;

- assess the risk to the child – this isn't seen as primarily the role of the adult mental health worker but often there is no one else in the position to carry out such an assessment.

The adult mental health worker's role in providing this information to other professionals and agencies is crucial. Communication is key.

Assessment of risk

There is public concern with safety, fuelled by press reports of attacks by mentally ill patients on strangers. In reality harm is much more likely to occur within one's own family. Dependency and the inability of small children to predict and avoid harm makes them particularly at risk. Five to 14 per cent of children under 16 are harmed. There are difficulties with determining when injuries, ill treatment and the standard of care fall below that expected of reasonable parents. Should mentally disordered parents be expected to meet higher standards than others? Clearer communication between mental health and childcare workers based on their respective knowledge and assessments might help to improve practice.

Chapter 10
Child and adolescent psychiatry

Most psychiatric disorders in childhood go untreated. Children are only referred to psychiatric services when their problems are a substantial burden to their parents or are interfering with schooling. The majority of children with psychiatric problems get no professional help at all. Some children, however, can access help from other sources such as primary health care, social services or youth offending teams.

The most common disorders referred to specialist psychiatric services are conduct disorder, anxiety disorders, depressive disorder and attention deficit hyperactivity disorder (ADHD).

Epidemiology

The main epidemiological studies in child psychiatry are the Isle of Wight and Inner London Borough studies (Rutter et al., 1970) which were conducted in the 1960s of 10- and 11-year-olds. The main findings have been confirmed by more recent studies, and include the following:

- The overall prevalence at any point in time of psychiatric disorder in the Isle of Wight was 7 per cent, twice that in Inner London.
- The most common disorders were conduct disorder and emotional disorders.
- Boys are twice as likely to be diagnosed with a psychiatric disorder as girls. The following diagnoses are more common in boys: pervasive developmental disorders (autism), ADHD, conduct disorder, tic disorder and completed suicide.
- Girls are more likely than boys to suffer from the following disorders: specific phobias, self-harm and depression in adolescence, and eating disorders.

Assessment

On assessing psychiatric disorders in childhood, information must be gathered from the child, the family and school. It is crucial to interview the child in a way that is developmentally appropriate. For example, with young children this can be done through drawing or play.

The assessment should ascertain the symptoms that the child presents in every domain including emotional and behavioural symptoms, developmental delays and relationship difficulties. The level of distress or impairment the disorder is causing to the child and the family, and any risks involved, should also be obtained.

It is also important to explore the family's strengths, beliefs and expectations, as the treatment plan should be built on these bases.

Attachment

Attachment theory

The term attachment was first described by Bowlby (1969) and refers to the need of a child to form close relationships to adult protective figures. The adult will act as a secure base from which to explore and as a safe place to retreat to when in danger or distress.

Attachment is crucial, as its quality predicts social and psychological development.

Attachment disorders

These refer to abnormal patterns of relationships with caregivers that develop before the age of 5 years. They are due to pathogenic care and cannot be explained by mental retardation or autistic spectrum disorders.

The ICD10 describes two types of attachment disorder:

- *Reactive*. The response to the caregiver can be inhibited, ambivalent or hypervigilant. The child avoids eye contact, lacks emotional responsiveness and resists comforting, but can be aggressive in response to their own or another's distress. The disorder is pervasive but typically reactive to changes in environmental circumstances, and it arises in relation to grossly inadequate care, typically abuse and neglect.

- *Disinhibited*. The child lacks selectivity for caregivers and characteristically presents with clingy behaviour in infancy and attention-seeking and indiscriminately friendly behaviour in early or middle childhood. The disorder arises due to marked discontinuities in caregivers (children raised in institutions) or multiple changes in family placements (multiple foster placements). The disorder tends to persist despite changes in environmental circumstances.

Pervasive developmental disorders: autism and Asperger's syndrome

Pervasive developmental disorders are a wide spectrum of social and language or communication disorders, including autism and Asperger's syndrome.

Two in 1,000 children have a pervasive developmental disorder and 10–15 per cent of this group have autism. This disorder is three times more frequent in boys than in girls.

Children with autism have three key features: social difficulties, communication difficulties and restricted, repetitive areas of interest and activities. The child usually is aloof, lacks empathy, can fail to seek comfort when hurt, has limited ability to form close friendships and has poor eye contact. They often get distressed with changes in routine.

Asperger's syndrome is a form of high functioning autism, usually with higher IQ and less language difficulties.

Early recognition of the disorder can help to address the needs of the child earlier, by, for instance, securing an adequate school placement, establishing support for parents, implementing behavioural programmes and organising respite care if necessary. Medication can be used with caution to manage associated symptoms such as hyperactivity or severe agitation.

Some studies of adopted children have showed that intense early life deprivation can present with social-communication difficulties similar to those seen in autism; however, they usually improve if the environment is favourable.

Attention deficit hyperactivity disorder

The prevalence of ADHD is 1–3 per cent and affects boys three times more than girls. It is believed to be more common in inner cities, low socio-economic families and children reared in institutions. The disorder is characterised by hyperactivity (fidgeting, restlessness), inattentiveness (reduced attention and concentration) and impulsiveness (social disinhibition, recklessness), which is pervasive across different settings (usually at home and at school). Referral to mental health services is often delayed until primary school though hyperactivity has generally already been observed in preschool.

Treatment options include:

- education and support to the children, parents and school;
- behavioural and parenting programmes to reinforce desired behaviour as well as cognitive techniques such us 'stop and think' commands;
- medication – many children respond well to stimulant medication such as methylphenidate, finding it easier to concentrate thus improving their academic performance and interaction with others which can improve their relationships with peers and their self-esteem;

There is little evidence on the beneficial effects of diet, although some parents report an improvement in their child's behaviour with the avoidance of certain foods such as additives or fizzy drinks.

Conduct disorder

Conduct disorder can be understood as a persistent failure to control behaviour appropriately within socially defined rules. It is the commonest child psychiatry disorder and affects more boys than girls. It is often persistent and causes a heavy cost to society. The clinical manifestations include defiance, aggressiveness and anti-social behaviour.

Genetic and environmental causes have been recognised. There is a strong association with child-rearing practices such as parental discord, hostility, lack of warmth towards the child, poor parental supervision and inconsistent discipline. Professionals working with these children need to be aware that some of them might have experienced some type of abuse.

Treatment

So far there is a lack of effective treatments although therapeutic work with the child and the parents can be beneficial. Treatment options include:

- behavioural therapy;
- problem solving;
- social skills training;
- parenting programmes;
- family work;
- social support.

Families frequently have difficult social circumstances, and motivation and consistency to engage in therapy can be compromised.

Eating disorders

The more salient disorders are anorexia nervosa and bulimia nervosa. Anorexia is characterised by self-induced weight loss (15 per cent below the expected weight) whereas in bulimia the weight is normal but there is an excessive preoccupation with weight control leading to repeated bouts of overeating and extreme measures to mitigate the fattening effects of food.

The prevalence of both conditions is low but both can have serious medical complications. Anorexia in particular has a high mortality risk. These conditions are more common in girls than in boys, and usually start in adolescence.

Genetic, environmental, psychological and personality factors are believed to play an important role in their aetiology.

Treatment

The main treatments involve weight restoration in anorexia with the elaboration of diet plans tailored to the needs of the patient together with graded physical activity. Current studies suggest that psychological therapies such as cognitive behavioural therapy and family therapy are the treatment of choice for these conditions. In some cases hospital admission might be necessary when the body weight is dangerously low, there are medical complications present such as dehydration, treatment in the community fails or there is a co-morbid psychiatric disorder like marked depression and suicidality.

Other disorders

Overall, children can suffer from the same major psychiatric conditions as adults although there is some variability in how they experience and express their distress.

Anxiety disorders

The three most common anxiety disorders are separation anxiety, generalised anxiety and specific phobias, followed by panic disorders, avoidant disorders, obsessive compulsive disorder and post-traumatic stress disorder (PTSD).

Mood disorders

The most common mood disorder in childhood is depression; mania or hypomania and bipolar disorders can occur but are rare.

Children with depression may present with a broad variety of symptoms including lack of energy, poor concentration, reduced appetite and disrupted sleeping pattern, hopelessness, guilt, low self-esteem, deliberate self-harm and suicidal thoughts. Specific manifestations such as restlessness, irritability and physical complaints such as abdominal pain and headaches should be taken into account. In the management of these children cognitive behavioural therapy, family work and school liaison are important treatments to consider and in the more severe cases the use of anti-depressant medication could be beneficial.

Psychotic disorders

These disorders are rare but can be a significant burden for the young person and the family. In child psychiatry the term first episode psychosis is frequently used rather than schizophrenia. It affects males and females the same but tends to present earlier in males. In most cases the psychotic symptoms (delusions and hallucinations) are preceded by a period in which families and others in close relation with the young person may have noticed changes in their behaviour such as social withdrawal and reduction in school performance. Early identification and optimal treatment can reduce the burden of the disorder and improve long-term outcome. The treatment options include the use of neuroleptic medication and psychosocial interventions such as family therapy, cognitive behavioural therapy and social support.

Treatment

The children and families that present to mental health services have complex problems that require complex solutions.

There is increasing emphasis in mental health settings to provide evidence-based interventions. The National Institute for Health and Clinical Excellence (NICE) provides clinical guidelines which are recommendations on the appropriate treatment and care of people with specific conditions within the NHS. The only specific guidelines in child and adolescent psychiatry are for the treatment of depression; however, NICE is currently developing new guidelines for ADHD and suspected child abuse.

Pharmacological treatments

Parents, teachers and mental health professionals often have reservations about the use of psychotropic medication with children; however, medication can be very beneficial if used at suitable doses and for appropriate conditions.

The same drugs used for adults (anti-depressants, mood stabilisers, benzodiazepines and neuroleptics) can be used with children, but due to the specific characteristics of the developing body of the child, they can have different effects and the doses vary. (See Chapter 16 for further discussion on the use of medication with children.)

Psychological treatments

Psychological interventions are widely used in child psychiatry. There is a range of interventions that can be used depending on the presenting problem. The most common are as follows:

- *Cognitive behavioural therapy (CBT)*. This aims to modify behaviours through changing the thoughts, mental schemas and feelings attached to them. This type of therapy is particularly useful in treating anxiety disorders and depression.

- *Psychodynamic psychotherapy*. This aims to achieve reintegration and change in personality functioning by the development of a deep interpersonal relationship between the child and the therapist that allows an analysis of past experiences and ways of coping. It is particularly used with children that have experienced trauma.

- *Family therapy*. Family systems have a strong influence in all members, and imbalances can present through problems in the child. Family therapy is used for a multitude of disorders.

Consent to treatment

The Gillick case established that a child under the age of 16 years can make the decision to have a medical treatment, if 'of sufficient understanding to make an informed decision'. However, a distinction must be made between consenting to have treatment versus deciding to refuse treatment. Thus while children may consent to have a treatment, they may not refuse. This even applies to children of 16 and 17. Parents that hold parental responsibility can provide consent for their children's treatment. The exception to this rule was introduced by the Mental Health Act 2007. Parents can no longer override the competent wishes of a 16- or 17-year-old when it comes to admission and treatment in a psychiatric hosptial.

The assessment of competence to give consent involves ascertaining whether the child is able to understand what has been proposed, its benefits and disadvantages, and the consequences of not having the treatment. The child's ability to retain the information given, to weigh up the information and to make a free choice should also be assessed.

Determining whether the child is competent should also take into account age, level of intelligence, degree of emotional maturity and whether the child's psychiatric condition affects his or her judgement. Even if not competent to consent, there is a value in obtaining the child's assent. (See Chapter 17 for more material on consent and capacity.)

Chapter 11

Treatment issues in psychiatry

There are three main aspects of psychiatric treatment:

- biological;

- psychological;

- social.

Other important issues relate to the selection of patients for treatment, the appropriate treatment for the condition, the treatability of the patient and the patient's consent. The aim of treatment in psychiatry, as in other branches of medicine, may be either:

- to contain present symptoms and prevent further deterioration; or

- to effect a cure and eradication of the original problem.

In most cases psychiatric treatment falls into the former category.

Biological treatments

Drugs

Drug treatment is widespread in psychiatry, particularly since the 1940s. Generally speaking the drugs prescribed for a psychiatric illness relate to the postulated abnormal biochemistry of the disorder, e.g. for schizophrenia it is postulated that an excess of dopamine in some areas of the brain is responsible for the characteristic psychotic symptoms. Pharmaceutical agents that lower levels of dopamine are prescribed to reduce the symptoms of schizophrenia. Drugs may also be prescribed to alleviate unpleasant symptoms, e.g. benzodiazepines (e.g. diazepam) for distressing symptoms of anxiety.

All new drugs are tested in laboratories first before they are tried on human subjects. The best way to assess whether a drug is effective is to perform a controlled trial where the assessors of the drug do not know if the subjects of the trial have had the drug or not ('blind'). All drugs have side effects most of which are known about by the time the drug comes to market and so appropriate warning can be given. Usually the patient and prescriber together weigh up the advantages/disadvantages of the drugs. There are, however, idiosyncratic responses that cannot be predicted.

The following chapters contain detailed information on drugs that are prescribed for mental disorders.

Electro-convulsive therapy

Discovered empirically in the 1920s and 1930s ECT is prescribed less than it was in the past. It is now used almost exclusively for the treatment of depression, especially where there is serious psychomotor retardation or there are delusions or strong suicidal intent. ECT is also indicated when a patient cannot tolerate drug treatment or where a quick response is needed. ECT is carried out under a general anaesthetic and is not painful. It does not change the personality or cause brain damage. In many cases there will be temporary amnesia post treatment and mild headache but otherwise ECT is free from side effects. This makes it distinct from the anti-depressants, and it is for this reason that ECT is still used. This includes its use with elderly patients who cannot tolerate medication or respond much more slowly.

In clinical trials, ECT has been shown to be effective in depression, i.e. it is better than no treatment at all and it is just as good as standard anti-depressants. The patient is given a short-acting anaesthetic. Oxygen is given, then a small amount of current given by electrodes is passed through the brain when the patient is anaesthetised in order to induce a fit. Muscle relaxation is given with the anaesthetic to reduce any muscular damage that might occur during the fit. The patient comes round from the anaesthetic in around five minutes; an anaesthetist and resuscitating equipment must be present in the room.

In order to administer ECT to someone without their consent, a second opinion from an independent psychiatrist must be obtained although in an emergency situation one ECT treatment can be administered to a detained patient if the grounds set out in section 62 of the Mental Health Act 1983 apply (see Brown, 2009, for more detail). The Mental Health Act 2007 introduced new safeguards for ECT. The main difficulty with ECT is that it frightens people, resembling a stereotype of treatment. Reassurance is an important part of therapy where ECT is given.

Psycho-surgery

Brain surgery to improve mental illness is now very rarely done in this country. The main indications are:

- severe obsessive–compulsive disorder;

- severe depression;

- severe anxiety.

Psycho-surgery is not now considered in order to control abnormally aggressive behaviour. Not only must the patient agree to the procedure but an independent psychiatrist plus two Mental Health Act Commissioners must also confirm that this is valid consent.

Psychological treatments

Psychological treatments focus on improving the patient's problems by communication and helping people to take their mental experiences seriously. Psychotherapy of various sorts may be combined with other treatments to provide a holistic package for the patient. Psychotherapy may be done individually, in pairs (marital therapy), in families or in groups. Psychotherapy falls into two main areas:

- behaviour-orientated psychotherapy;
- person- or relationship-orientated psychotherapy.

Behaviour-orientated psychotherapy

This aims to change behaviour where it has become unacceptable or disadvantageous to the patient, e.g. phobias about animals or public transport. Behaviour therapy focuses on how to reduce the frequency of the behaviour by setting goals and targets and looking for ways of reinforcing different behaviours from the unwanted one. In behaviour therapy a contract is usually drawn up between the therapist and the patient and therapist and patient are on equal terms. The responsibility to cure lies with the patient and the therapist is a guide rather than a traditional healer. Behaviour therapy is extremely effective in certain types of conditions but is not effective in others.

A variation on behaviour therapy is *cognitive therapy*. This is the application of behaviour therapy principles to negative thoughts that the patient may have. In cognitive therapy sessions, disadvantageous thoughts/beliefs will be explored and challenged and those thoughts that are advantageous are reinforced. Cognitive therapy is used most often in the treatment of mild depression, where it is as effective as anti-depressants.

Person-orientated psychotherapy

This ranges from psychoanalysis at one extreme to self-help groups like Alcoholics Anonymous at the other. Between the two extremes lie varying types of therapy with different theoretical constructs underlying the process. Differences between different types of psychotherapy relate to the timing of sessions, the length of sessions, the frequency of sessions, the content of the sessions with reference to the therapist's activity or lack of it and the expectations of the therapist–patient alliance. For example, psychoanalysis is based on the theories of Freud and patients' problems will be seen according to this model. Such patients tend to be intelligent, articulate, motivated and middle class enough to pay for therapy. In general they suffer from neurotic problems and come for 50-minute sessions every day. In the session, the patient free associates and the therapist says very little except to describe patterns or thoughts in the patient's speech. In contrast, Alcoholics Anonymous is a group therapy with no therapist. Group members come from all walks of life and funding is based on minimal donations. There is a strict theoretical model applied that group members explore in discussion. There is also an emphasis on group support.

Does psychotherapy work? The answer is emphatically 'yes'. But like all medical treatments, the right therapy needs to be tailored to the patient's problems. Phobias are best dealt with by behaviour therapy, but behaviour therapy is unlikely to be useful for complicated grief reactions. Patients demand for psychotherapy in the NHS exceeds availability, especially for ethnic minorities and long-term problems such as personality disorder. Many criticisms can be made of psychotherapy; however, most patients see it as being what a psychiatrist should do for them – 'someone to talk to'. Psychotherapy is about change; it is indicated for those patients who wish to change something about themselves or their behaviour. The responsibility for change lies with the patient and it is almost impossible to have psychotherapy against one's will.

Social or environmental treatments

There are no formalised treatments that a psychiatrist can prescribe in this area but it is important to remember that as part of the treatment programme, issues like housing and occupation are extremely important in terms of the patient's functioning in society and self-respect. Important community examples are befriending and rehabilitation schemes. Sheltered workshops and therapeutic hostel placements are also important from this point of view. This is particularly an issue with 'difficult patients' who are not liked by medical and social services but are still very much in need. Therapeutic communities, like the Henderson Hospital in Sutton, South London, are an example of a treatment where the milieu is the therapy.

Chapter 12
Classification of medication in psychiatry

Introduction to medication in psychiatry

For full prescribing information on any drug including special precautions, drug interactions, indications and contra-indications the reader should refer to the latest edition of the *British National Formulary* (*BNF*) or the Summary of Product Characteristics (SPC/Data Sheet). The BNF is updated every six months and is fully indexed.

At the time of going to print the current *BNF* is Volume 57 dated March 2009. This is available from bookshops or online at: www.bnf.org/bnf.

It is free to register online with the *BNF* so this is the easiest way to obtain accurate up-to-date information. Please note that while principal brand names for drugs are given in brackets, many agents are available in generic form or as other brands. Please consult the latest *British National Formulary* for further clarification.

Drug names now reflect the new rINN (recommended International Non-proprietary Name) which supersedes the former BAN (British Approved Name). Where the two differ the former BAN is given in lower case in adjacent parentheses. All dispensed medication labels now adopt rINN nomenclature.

British National Formulary classification headings

Chapter 4 of the BNF is the key chapter for drugs used in psychiatry. It uses the system of classification as set out below. This is often used on forms T2 and T3 which cover consent to treatment procedures for patients detained under the Mental Health Act 1983. For example, a second opinion appointed doctor (SOAD) appointed by the Core Quality Commission might enter at the foot of Form T3 (covering treatment when the patient has withheld consent or has been unable to give valid consent – section 58) something like: 'up to two drugs in 4.2.1 given orally up to *BNF* limits'.

With Form T2 (where the Approved Clinician has obtained valid consent from the patient) the doctor may well record the actual name of the drug rather than the BNF classification. This is consistent with the Code of Practice and may well be more helpful for the patient who is more likely to have consented to a specific drug rather than a *BNF* classification.

Some relevant extracts from the English Code of Practice concerning medication

24.13 *Section 58 applies only to detained patients. They cannot be given medication to which section 58 applies unless:*

- *the approved clinician in charge of the treatment, or a SOAD, certifies that the patient has the capacity to consent and has done so; or*

- *a SOAD certifies that the treatment is appropriate and either that:*
  - *the patient does not have the capacity to consent; or*
  - *the patient has the capacity to consent but has refused to do so.*

24.14 *Hospital managers should ensure that systems are in place to remind both the clinician in charge of the medication and the patient at least four weeks before the expiry of the three-month period.*

24.15 *Warning systems must be capable of dealing with the possibility that a patient may become an SCT patient, and may also have their community treatment order revoked, during the three-month period. A patient's move between detention and SCT does not change the date on which the three-month period expires.*

24.16 *Where approved clinicians certify the treatment of a patient who consents, they should not rely on the certificate as the only record of their reasons for believing that the patient has consented to the treatment. A record of their discussion with the patient, and of the steps taken to confirm that the patient has the capacity to consent, should be made in the patient's notes as normal.*

24.17 *Certificates under this section must clearly set out the specific forms of treatment to which they apply. All the relevant drugs should be listed, including medication to be given 'as required' (prn), either by name or by the classes described in the* British National Formulary (BNF). *If drugs are specified by class, the certificate should state clearly the number of drugs authorised in each class, and whether any drugs within the class are excluded. The maximum dosage and route of administration should be clearly indicated for each drug or category of drugs proposed. This can exceed the dosages listed in the* BNF, *but particular care is required in these cases.*

British National Formulary *classification headings*

4.1 Hypnotics and anxiolytics	*4.1.1 Hypnotics*
	4.1.2 Anxiolytics
	4.1.3 Barbiturates

4.2 Drugs used in psychoses
      and related disorders

4.2.1 Anti-psychotic drugs

4.2.2 Anti-psychotic depot injections

4.2.3 Anti-manic drugs

4.3 Anti-depressant drugs

4.3.1 Tricyclic and related anti-depressant drugs

4.3.2 Monoamine-oxidase inhibitors (MAOIs)

4.3.3 SSRIs and related anti-depressants

4.3.4 Other anti-depressant drugs

4.4 Central nervous stimulants

4.4   Central nervous stimulants

4.5 Drugs used in the treatment of
      obesity

4.5.1 Anti-obesity drugs acting on gastro-
        intestinal tract

4.5.2 Centrally acting appetite suppressants

4.6 Drugs used in nausea and vertigo

4.6   Drugs used in nausea and vertigo

4.7 Analgesics

4.7.1 Non-opioid analgesics

4.7.2 Opioid analgesics

4.7.3 Neuropathic pain

4.7.4 Anti-migraine drugs

4.8 Anti-epileptics

4.8.1 Control of epilepsy

4.8.2 Drugs used in status epilepticus

4.8.3 Febrile convulsions

4.9 Drugs used in parkinsonism and
      related disorders

4.9.1 Dopaminergic drugs used in
        parkinsonism

4.9.2 Anti-muscarinic drugs used in
        parkinsonism

4.9.3 Drugs used in essential tremor, chorea,
        tics and related disorders

4.10 Drugs used in substance dependence

4.11 Drugs for dementia

Chapter 13
Anti-depressants and mood stabilisers

Anti-depressants (*BNF* section 4.3)

There are principally three core groups of antidepressant drugs available. These are divided on the basis of either their mechanism of action (MAOIs and SSRIs) or their chemical structure (TCAs).

Monoamine oxidase inhibitors (MAOIs)

Phenelzine	(Nardil)
Isocarboxazid	(Marplan)
Tranylcypromine	(Parnate)

Reversible inhibitors of monoamine oxidase A (RIMAs)

Moclobemide	(Manerix)

Tricyclic anti-depressants (TCAs)

Amitriptyline	(Lentizol)
Imipramine	(Tofranil)
Trimipramine	(Surmontil)
Protriptyline	(Concordin)
Dosulepin (dothiepin)	(Prothiaden)
Clomipramine	(Anafranil)
Doxepin	(Sinequan)
Amoxapine	(Asendis)
Lofepramine	(Gamanil)

Selective serotonin re-uptake inhibitors (SSRIs)

Fluvoxamine	(Faverin)
Sertraline	(Lustral)

Fluoxetine	(Prozac)
Citalopram	(Cipramil)
Paroxetine	(Seroxat)
Escitalopram*	(Cipralex)

* This compound is the active portion (isomer) of citalopram and was introduced in its own right in July 2002. Compared to citalopram it requires only half the dosage for equivalent effect, but the manufacturer's claimed superiority over Eitalopram is not generally accepted. It is not considered a cost-effective first-line treatment for depression given the cheaper alternative of generic SSRIs.

Other anti-depressants

These agents have a more complex mechanism of action and include some of the new compounds:

Mianserin

Venlafaxine	(Efexor)
Maprotiline	(Ludiomil)
Mirtazapine	(Zispin)
Trazodone	(Molipaxin)
Reboxetine	(Edronax)
Duloxetine	(Cymbalta)
L-Tryptophan	(Optimax)

Use of anti-depressants

Anti-depressants are principally used to combat the signs and symptoms of depression but do have other uses. Outside of mental health some of the older agents, e.g. amitriptyline, may be used for control of nerve pain and in children to help with night-time bedwetting. Apart from helping to relieve depression some of the older sedative agents, e.g. amitriptyline and dosulepin, are used in low doses for night sedation alone. This represents an unlicensed use and is not recommended because of the additional unwanted effects when compared to the pure sedative/hypnotic (sleeping tablets) group.

The SSRIs may be used for a range of anxiety spectrum conditions such as panic attacks, eating disorders, obsessive compulsive disorder (OCD), post-traumatic stress disorder (PTSD), phobic disorders and social anxiety disorder.

Clinical practice points

All anti-depressants take 4–6 weeks to achieve maximum benefit in depression. Generally adverse effects will predominate during the first week with little therapeutic gain until about week two.

After response has been achieved it is important to continue with the medication for at least six months. This maintenance period may be extended if there is a history of previous episodes of depression or ongoing stress factors.

Anti-depressants are *not* addictive but many patients require this to be said or they may cease treatment prematurely. Unless only a few weeks of medication has been taken anti-depressants should be reduced gradually to minimise the occurrence of *discontinuation reactions*. A tapering-off over 3–4 weeks is usually adequate but some agents (e.g. paroxetine) are more prone to discontinuation effects than others.

Discontinuation reactions can be distinguished from a recurrence of depression by their rapid resolution following reintroduction of the anti-depressant.

How do anti-depressants work?

The brain chemicals (transmitters) associated with mood and other biological factors that are changed in depression are dopamine, noradrenaline and serotonin (5-HT). Of these three serotonin has attracted most interest and has a whole group of anti-depressants invested in it (SSRIs). All anti-depressants seek to promote the activity of one or more of these transmitters at a key site of action usually defined as a receptor. Over the years the ways in which this goal is achieved by newer anti-depressants has got more complex and it is now not so easy to correlate the pharmacology directly with clinical observations.

Adverse effects

A number of adverse effects are group specific and can be predicted from known pharmacological action. These are set out in Table 13.1.

Table 13.1 Side effects of anti-depressants

MAOIs	TCAs	SSRIs
Dose titration required	**Dose titration required**	Start at therapeutic dose
Insomnia	Many are very sedative	Minimal sedation
Do not take last dose after teatime	Risk of accidents/falls due to next-day drowsiness	Alerting effects leading to feeling more on edge for 1–2 weeks
AVOID TYRAMINE	**Anti-cholinergic effects**	**Nausea for 1–2 weeks**
Special leaflet warning about interactions needed	Dry mouth	Headache
	Blurred vision	
	Constipation	
	Confusion (elderly)	
	Urinary retention	
Postural hypotension	Postural hypotension	Minimal hypotension
Sexual dysfunction	Sexual dysfunction	Sexual dysfunction
Toxic in overdose	**Toxic in overdose**	Little acute toxicity
Cheap	Cheap	Cheap if prescribed generically
Caution with alcohol	**Caution with alcohol**	Minimal interaction with alcohol
Lowering of seizure threshold	Lowering of seizure threshold	Lowering of seizure threshold
Weight gain	Weight gain	Weight gain (except fluoxetine)

Other Anti-depressants

Moclobemide does not require the strict MAOI precautions that apply to the traditional MAOIs.

Maprotiline has a profile midway between TCAs and SSRIs but a higher incidence of seizures. It is little used nowadays.

Mianserin has a high degree of sedation and full blood counts must be carried out monthly during the first three months of therapy to check for anaemia. Only available as a generic drug. Largely superseded by mirtazapine.

Venlafaxine (SNRI) has a side-effect profile similar to SSRIs but a mechanism of action more closely resembling the TCAs affecting re-uptake of both noradrenaline and 5-HT. High doses may be employed in more difficult cases to treat patients but above 200 mg daily blood pressure should be checked for possible hypertension. Caution is required for patients with pre-existing cardiac disease and pre-existing raised blood pressure. ECG monitoring was required in all patients (NICE, 2004) until repealed by the Medicines and Healthcare Products Regulatory Agency (MHRA) in 2006.

Duloxetine (SNRI) represents the second SNRI agent. Given as a single once-daily dose the main side effects are nausea, dry mouth and constipation. It possesses analgesic properties like some of the early tricyclics but with little other receptor baggage. It is also separately licensed for stress incontinence as Yentreve.

Trazodone has marked anxiety-relieving properties but causes unpleasant dizziness if taken on an empty stomach due to its rapid absorption. Priapism can be a problem in male patients.

Mirtazapine (NaSSA) offers the profile of the SSRIs but without the early nausea and alerting effects. It also produces less sexual dysfunction but has a high incidence of weight gain and early sedation may be unhelpful for some patients.

Reboxetine (NARI) is totally noradrenaline-focused in its mechanism of action and provides greatest benefit in the very withdrawn, anergic patient. Insomnia and dry mouth are the chief complaints with this compound.

L-tryptophan is a naturally occurring amino acid precursor of serotonin and in large doses (3–6 g daily) exhibits anti-depressant activity. It became a popular adjunctive treatment due to its better adverse-effect profile than many of the then current anti-depressants (nausea was the only significant adverse effect). In the late 1980s a number of patients developed an eosinophilia myalgia syndrome (EMS). This syndrome is characterised by a marked increase in the eosinophil count and muscle pain together with fever, skin rash and oedema. Occasionally lung and nervous system tissues may be affected producing respiratory failure and polyneuropathy. EMS was almost certainly a reaction to a contaminant in one of the raw materials but nevertheless from then until February 2005 in order to use this product both the prescribing doctor and patient had to be registered with the company's OPTICS scheme (Optimax Information and Clinical Support).

OPTICS registration was rescinded on 14 February 2005.

Mood stabilisers (*BNF* section 4.2.3)

The term mood stabiliser is used to describe medicines that are taken on a prophylactic basis (i.e. in a preventative way) to protect against mood swings.

The principal agents are lithium carbonate and the anti-convulsant carbamazepine but many of the newer anti-convulsant (anti-epileptic) drugs are used as alternatives particularly where there is poor response or tolerability problems to these first-line drugs. Sodium Valproate is now a popular choice but it should be noted that none of these alternative agents is licensed for chronic use in bipolar/manic depression illness.

Lithium carbonate

Lithium carbonate tablets   (Camcolit, Priadel, Liskonum)

Lithium citrate   (Litarex, Li-liquid, Priadel liquid)

Lithium may also be used to augment an anti-depressant in patients with unipolar depression.

Dosing information
Lithium has a narrow therapeutic range meaning that there is only a small difference between the therapeutic and toxic dose.

Blood tests form an integral part of lithium management and therapeutic levels are in the range 0.4–1.0 mmol/litre. Blood samples are taken 12 hours after the last dose and sampling is easiest if the patient takes their lithium as a single daily dose at night.

Side effects
Early on in treatment there are a number of predictable and classic side effects:

- polydipsia (increased thirst);

- polyuria (increased urine output);

- mild stomach discomfort with some looseness of the bowels;

- fine tremor of the hands.

These early effects usually settle within 1–2 weeks with the person adapting to the increased urine output. In the medium term lithium levels should be checked every three months and kidney and thyroid function on an annual basis Some patients may notice a swelling in the neck (goitre). Lithium can reduce the output of thyroid hormone but this is easily corrected with levothyroxine. Often any reduction in thyroid activity is picked up by blood tests before the patient notices any discomfort.

Weight gain is a significant side effect of lithium therapy.

Monitoring in the long term should include routine lithium levels on a 3-monthly basis and checks on renal function and thyroid status 6-monthly or at least annually. Shared care guidelines may well be in place between the specialist mental health services and primary care and these will spell out working details and rules and responsibilities for safe medicines management of lithium.

Lithium toxicity

When levels exceed 1.5 mmol/l signs of lithium toxicity begin to develop. Lithium toxicity is characterised by:

• severe shaking of the hands

• giddiness or loss of balance

• slurred speech

• unusual sleepiness or slowness

• vomiting or diarrhoea

and should be classed as a medical emergency.

Lithium levels may become high unintentionally, and usually the cause will be one of three reasons. It is important to educate the patient on avoiding lithium toxicity.

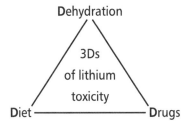

Dehydration – extreme fluid loss due to feverish illness, sickness and diarrhoea, etc., should prompt a stopping of the lithium until the patient is better to avoid high concentrations of lithium developing.

Diet – extreme changes to salt intake, particularly the exclusion of salt from the diet, may lead to the body retaining more lithium to compensate for the salt loss.

Drugs – some medications may interact with lithium to push levels into the toxic range. This applies not just to prescription drugs where the water tablet bendroflumethiazide is a classic example but also to some counter medications such as ibuprofen (Neurofen) which is best avoided unless there is good access to close monitoring of the lithium.

The *BNF* should be consulted for further advice, and patients advised to ask their pharmacist before purchasing any over-the-counter remedies.

Other issues

Lithium, like many other psychotropic drugs, is designed to be taken long term and does not lead to addiction and dependence.

Small amounts of alcohol are safe but plenty of other fluids should be taken to avoid dehydration.

Carbamazepine

Carbamazepine   (Tegretol, Tegretol Retard)

The three principal uses of carbamazepine are

- as a mood stabiliser;
- for the treatment of epilepsy;
- to help with pain management in trigeminal neuralgia (one-sided facial pain).

Blood level monitoring is generally employed when carbamazepine is used in the treatment of epilepsy and therapeutic levels are quoted as 4–12 mg/l (20–50 micromol/l). These levels are trough levels and blood samples should be taken just before the next dose of the drug is due. This therapeutic range has not been proven for mood stabilising activity.

Unless toxicity is suspected carbamazepine assays should not be undertaken until two weeks after any dosage change because levels are not stable before then.

Carbamazepine can cause anaemia and it is recommended that full blood counts are carried out on an annual basis

Side effects
Dizziness and drowsiness often limit large dosage increases and small increments made at 1–2 weekly intervals can minimise these problems. Large doses given less frequently than smaller doses more often is attractive regarding compliance but may give rise to unacceptable side effects from high peak levels.

Blurred vision or double vision is a sign that blood levels may be too high and a revisit of the dosing regimen may be worthwhile. The use of the Retard preparation can sometimes be helpful in preserving less frequent dosing.

About one in ten patients can develop skin rashes. This is an indication for stopping the drug.

Other practice points
Carbamazepine is subject to numerous drug interactions. Some medications will increase levels of carbamazepine itself while in other circumstances carbamazepine itself speeds up the metabolism of the other drug.

When new drugs are introduced alongside carbamazepine it is worth checking the latest *BNF* to see if any action is needed.

Other anti-convulsants

The following anti-convulsants may be encountered as unlicensed products in the chronic management of bipolar disorders:

Sodium valproate   (Epilim)

Valproate semi sodium   (Depakote)

There is a growing amount of evidence to support the use of valproate in bipolar disorders and the drug is used first line in USA where it is available as Depakote or Divalproex. Depakote is available in the UK with a license for *acute* mania. When first launched Depakote was much more expensive than conventional sodium valproate and felt by many to offer no real advantages, so it may not be in routine clinical practice in your area. Sodium valproate delivers around 30 per cent lower peak valproate levels than Depakote but in clinical practice 1:1 dosing conversion is considered acceptable. In bipolar disorder effective valproate doses are around 500 mg three times a day. Blood level monitoring is generally not that helpful in clinical management due to fluctuating levels. Common adverse effects with valproate include gastro-intestinal upset with nausea and occasional vomiting. Supporters of Depakote claim that this formulation is better tolerated but weight gain with increased appetite will affect a significant number of patients.

Transient scalp hair loss with (sometimes curly) regrowth within six months is also associated with this drug. Although rare, serious blood and liver disorders can occur with this drug and indications for stopping treatment include spontaneous bruising or bleeding and jaundice accompanied with malaise, weakness and lethargy. Severe abdominal pain and vomiting may indicate pancreatitis and urgent medical referral should be sought.

See also:

Vigabatrin   (Sabril)

Topiramate   (Topamax)

Gabapentin   (Neurontin)

Lamotrigine   (Lamictal)

The latest NICE guidance (Clinical Guidance no. 38, 2006) on the management of bipolar disorder recognises the increasing role lamotrigine can play in treating bipolar depression. Lamotrigine should be introduced gradually to minimise the risk of provoking a skin reaction. Skin reactions may progress to much more serious forms of allergic type reaction. The titration process needs to be 50 per cent slower if the patient is on valproate due to valproate doubling lamotrigine levels. Lamotrigine itself is generally well tolerated and requires no blood level monitoring or other blood tests in its own right.

Chapter 14
Anti-psychotics
(*BNF* section 4.2)

Anti-psychotics are sometimes referred to as neuroleptics or major tranquillisers. These titles should be regarded as outdated in modern clinical practice.

The early anti-psychotics are collectively known as conventional or typical anti-psychotics while the term *atypical* anti-psychotic has been coined to reflect the improved side-effect and quality profile that many of the newer agents possess.

Phenothiazines		Butyrophenones	
Chlorpromazine	(Largactil)	Haloperidol	(Haldol, Serenace)
Thioridazine*	(Melleril)	Benperidol	(Anquil)
Trifluoperazine	(Stelazine)		
Perphenazine	(Fentazin)		
Prochlorperazine	(Stemetil)		
Promazine			

* Thioridazine is restricted to second line use in adults with schizophrenia because of concern over its potential cardiotoxicity. It is no longer available in the UK.

Thioxanthenes		Other conventional anti-psychotics	
Zuclopenthixol	(Clopixol)	Pimozide	(Orap)
Flupentixol	(Depixol)	Sulpiride	(Dolmatil, Sulptil, Sulparex)

Anti-psychotic depot injections

Fluphenazine decanoate	(Modecate)
Flupentixol decanoate	(Depixol)
Haloperidol decanoate	(Haldol)
Pipotiazine palmitate	(Piportil)
Zuclopenthixol decanoate	(Clopixol)
Zuclopenthixol acetate	(Clopixol Acuphase)

Atypical anti-psychotics

Amisulpride	(Solian)	
Aripiprazole	(Abilify)	
Clozapine	(Clozaril)	
Olanzapine	(Zyprexa)	
Paliperidone	(Invega)	
Quetiapine	(Seroquel)	
Risperidone	(Risperdal)	Risperidone Consta (long-acting injection)
Zotepine	(Zoleptil)	

Uses of anti-psychotics

- *Anti-psychotic* – in this capacity they reduce the positive symptoms of psychotic illness such as hearing voices (hallucinations), strange thinking and unrealistic beliefs (delusions).

- *Anxiolytic* – low doses of the more sedative agents are used in non-psychotic situations to reduce high stress levels, e.g. promazine for reducing agitation in the elderly.

- *Anti-emetic* – a number of the anti-psychotics have anti-sickness properties and are used in this respect in special circumstances, e.g. haloperidol in palliative care and prochlorperazine (Stemetil) in routine medical practice.

- *Analgesia* – the pain-killing properties of the older anti-psychotics are sometimes used by specialist pain clinics in the management of difficult to treat nerve pain.

As part of a ***rapid tranquillisation programme*** when the oral route is not available the atypical anti-psychotics Olanzapine and Aripiprazole are the preferred options for neuroleptic naive patients.

High-dose conventional anti-psychotics should be avoided in the management of acutely disturbed patients as they have been associated with sudden death. The Royal College of Psychiatrists consensus statement on the use of high-dose anti-psychotic medicines updated in 2006 provides further guidance on this topic.

Clopixol Acuphase is a short-acting conventional depot designed for acute management of high arousal states resulting from psychotic illness. It should be used under close supervision as its effects cannot be quickly terminated.

Benzodiazepines such as lorazepam IM or diazepam (Diazemuls) IV provide resolution of high arousal states and are acutely much safer compounds, although close monitoring of any patients undergoing IM rapid tranquillisation is necessary with attention to vital signs and access to resuscitation facilities and medical support

Most trusts will have their own Rapid Tranquillisation Protocol but there is an excellent flowchart in the summary NICE guidance on managing violence (Clinical Guidance No. 25, February 2005).

How do anti-psychotics work?

It is believed that over-activity of the chemical messenger dopamine in specific regions of the brain accounts for many of the features of a psychotic illness.

Anti-psychotics reduce the activity of dopamine by blocking its receptor sites. Many areas of the brain require dopamine to function normally and the reduction of dopamine activity in the motor area of the brain (extrapyramidal tract) accounts for the movement-related side effects commonly referred to as EPS. The newer atypical anti-psychotics have a more refined pharmacology achieved by additional activity at other transmitter sites.

Unwanted EPS effects

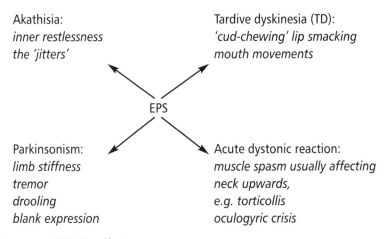

Akathisia:
inner restlessness
the 'jitters'

Tardive dyskinesia (TD):
'cud-chewing' lip smacking
mouth movements

EPS

Parkinsonism:
limb stiffness
tremor
drooling
blank expression

Acute dystonic reaction:
muscle spasm usually affecting
neck upwards,
e.g. torticollis
oculogyric crisis

Figure 14.1 *Extrapyramidal side effects*

Management of acute EPS

Anti-cholinergic agents can be used to reverse the symptoms of parkinsonism and acute dystonic reaction.

These drugs are effective because the dopamine deficiency in the motor area of the brain results in excess of another transmitter compound called acetylcholine. Anti-cholinergics reduce the amount of acetylcholine and restore an equilibrium between dopamine and acetylcholine.

The anti-cholinergic drugs are in section 4.9.2 of the *BNF* and include:

Procyclidine	(Kemadrin)
Orphenadrine	(Disipal)
Trihexphenidyl (benzhexol)	(Artane)
Benzatropine (benztropine)	(Cogentin)

For ***parkinsonism*** oral anti-cholinergics are titrated upwards to a dose that abolishes the EPS. Prophylactic dosing or extra dosing should not be used as these drugs have an abuse potential, carry their own baggage of side effects and in large doses can precipitate a psychosis.

For ***acute dystonic reactions*** the anti-cholinergic should be given by injection: 10 mg IM of procyclidine is the standard dose.

For ***akathisia***, anti-cholinergics have little benefit and optimum management involves a dose reduction or move to a lower potency agent. This may well involve substituting with an atypical anti-psychotic. Propranolol (a beta blocker) may benefit some patients by reducing the physical components of the restlessness.

Tardive dyskinesia is a late onset EPS and is made worse by anti-cholinergics. Any existing anti-cholinergics should be gradually withdrawn and anti-psychotic medication reviewed. Atypical anti-psychotics show reduced incidence of TD but established TD does not respond rapidly to any intervention.

Common side effects of anti-cholinergics include

- dry mouth;

- blurred vision;

- constipation.

A number of patients find that anti-cholinergics can provide a 'buzz' and these agents do carry some abuse potential.

Other adverse effects of anti-psychotics include the following:

- *Hormonal effects*. Raised prolactin accounts for irregular periods and lactation (production of breast milk) as well as sexual difficulties in both males and females. Long term, raised prolactin can be a risk factor for brittle bones (osteoporosis).

- *Weight gain/metabolic syndrome*. Many of the drugs used in psychiatry produce problematic weight gain. Among the anti-psychotics the phenothiazines both stimulate appetite and slow down metabolism. Increases in fasting glucose levels and worsening lipid profiles have been identified with some atypical anti-psychotics although it is accepted that a severe and enduring mental illness carries a higher incidence of type 2 diabetes and cardiovascular morbidity. Hence there is now much emphasis on monitoring the physical health care needs of all clients with severe and enduring mental health problems.

- *Cardiovascular system*. Postural hypotension leading to dizziness on standing can be particularly problematic in the elderly leading to increased risk of falls and accidents. Patients should be advised to get up slowly after sitting or lying down. Anti-psychotics are known to affect cardiac conduction through prolongation of QTc interval. In rare instances this may lead to serious cardiac arrythmias. Thioridazine and pimozide carry the highest risk, although you are unlikely to encounter these medications nowadays

- *Skin reactions*. Chlorpromazine represents an increased risk of sunburn and all patients should apply high protection sunscreen (combined UVA and B protection 30+) before going out into strong daylight.

Atypical anti-psychotics

Table 14.1 *Comparison of atypical anti-psychotics*

Drug presentation	EPS	Sedation	Postural hypotension	Raised prolactin	Weight gain	Clinical practice
Amisulpride (Solian) T, L	+	0	0	++	+	A close relative of sulpiride with low doses indicated for relief of negative symptoms. Minimal weight gain but raised prolactin is often problematic.
Aripiprazole (Abilify) T Odis, L, IM	0+	0	0	0	0+	Unique as a partial agonist at dopamine receptors. Clean profile may be let down by significant headache/nausea/vomiting, and minimal sedation may prompt insomnia. Although low EPS, akathisia has been noted. Good metabolic profile and cognitive gains.
Olanzapine (Zyprexa) T, Odis, IM	0+	+	0	0+	+++	No initial dosage titration required. Few drug interactions. Some sedation. Weight gain often problematic. Cited as higher incidence of diabetes/metabolic syndrome. Impacts positively on cognition, suicidality and reduced inpatient stays.
Quetiapine (Seroquel) T	0	++	++	0	+	Similar properties to olanzapine but dosage titration required to minimise postural hypotension. Least effect on prolactin levels.
Risperidone (Risperdal) T, Odis, L, D	Dose dependent above 6 mg/day	0	++	++	++	Dosage titration required. Less sedative than olanzapine. Weight gain and raised prolactin may be problematic for some patients. Watch for dose emergent EPS. Economic gains similar to olanzapine.
Paliperidone T						Paliperidone is an active metabolite (byproduct) of risperidone marketed in its own right with some improvement in tolerability profile when compared with risperidone itself.
Zotepine (Zoleptil) T	+	++	+++	+	+	Little used; atypical with dizziness and postural hypotension main adverse effects. Patients at risk of arrythmias should have ECG. Doses above 300 mg daily significantly increase risk of fits. No clear niche.
Clozapine (Clozaril, Zaponex, Denzapine) T	0	+++	+++	0	+++	*For treatment refractory patients only.* Registration with company's monitoring system required. Close haematological monitoring required while on medication. Excessive dribbling can be helped by *Kwells*. Lowers seizure threshold and if epileptic activity develops sodium valproate is anti-convulsant of choice. Avoid carbamazepine or phenothiazines as these can increase chance of neutropoenia.

Key: T = tablet, L = liquid, D = depot (long-acting injection), IM = short-acting injection, Odis = orodispersible tablet (melt formulation), 0 = no effect, + = positive effect (strength indicated by number of crosses).

Atypical anti-psychotics

(See Table 14.1 for a summary.)

Apart from the side effects already covered many patients find that the older conventional anti-psychotics cause a high degree of unwanted flattening or dysphoria prompting comments such as 'makes me feel like a zombie'. This coupled with the negative symptoms of schizophrenia serves only to further reduce initiative and drive and worsen motivation.

The atypical anti-psychotics represent some improvement in this area. Appropriately quantified as a 'refinement not a revolution' many patients feel stronger and brighter on these agents although there may be little difference in impact on the positive symptoms of the illness.

Atypical anti-psychotics represent a big increase in drug costs, from around £100 per year for drugs such as haloperidol to upwards of £2,000 for an atypical agent.

Even with this increase in drug costs, medication still accounts for around only 6 per cent of the treatment costs of someone with schizophrenia.

Additional medication costs may be offset by a reduction in days spent in hospital, a return to work and therefore less benefit claims and a reduction in suicides.

Data in these areas are currently strongest for clozapine.

In early 2002 NICE reviewed the evidence around atypical anti-psychotics and recommended that:

- atypicals are the anti-psychotics of choice for first episode psychosis;
- patients who have tolerability problems with existing typical drugs should be assessed for the use of an atypical;
- clozapine should be offered as soon as treatment refractoriness is evident.

Risperidone is the first atypical agent to become available in depot form (August 2002). Known as Risperdal Consta it is *not* an oily based injection but comes as a dry powder requiring reconstitution prior to administration. *It must be stored in a refrigerator. Part doses from a vial cannot be administered.*

Risperdal Consta has a delayed release profile equating to a three-week void before *any* therapeutic amounts of drug are released. Hence oral anti-psychotic medication is needed during the titration phase. Dosing interval is two-weekly and dosages should commence at 25 mg two-weekly increasing to a maximum of 50 mg two-weekly if necessary. There is little value in routinely exceeding this upper dose.

The costs of using this depot are in line with atypical anti-psychotic treatment.

Chapter 15
Anxiolytics and sedative/hypnotics (*BNF* section 4.1)

Benzodiazepines

At the height of the benzodiazepine era there were 21 compounds available worldwide and some 15 on the UK market. In the mid-1980s the government applied restrictions through blacklisting making around half of them not allowable on NHS prescription.

Special listing also prohibits NHS prescribing by brand name but many patients still use the original patent names when describing these agents.

Benzodiazepines essentially share *four* properties mediated through the complex benzodiazepine receptors located in the central nervous system:

- anxiolytic (anxiety reducing);
- sedative (tranquillising properties which in larger doses will induce sleep);
- anti-convulsant (for treating epilepsy, e.g. clobazam and clonazepam);
- muscle relaxant (usually diazepam itself).

Tradition has to some extent dictated which benzodiazepines are applied where.

Anxiolytic benzodiazepines		Hypnotic benzodiazepines	
Diazepam	(Valium)	Temazepam	
Chlordiazepoxide	(Librium)	Nitrazepam	(Mogadon)
Lorazepam	(Ativan)	Lormetazepam	
Oxazepam		Loprazolam	
		Flunitrazepam	non-NHS ('roofers')

Benzodiazepines began to take over from the very toxic barbiturate compounds in the 1960s and represented much cleaner and safer drugs with very few side effects and little serious toxicity if alcohol was taken alongside.

It is now recognised that while benzodiazepines may offer quick relief from acute stress their continued use leads to dependence and some loss of efficacy. Currently chronic use of these medications is licensed for a maximum of four weeks. For patients who have been taking benzodiazepines for many years careful reduction programmes can enable successful withdrawal but no one should stop long-term benzodiazepines abruptly as the rebound effects can be very distressing both psychologically and physically.

It is also now appreciated that benzodiazepines suppress not only negative stressful feelings but can also impair the capacity for enjoyment and the learning of healthy coping skills.

Other sedative/hypnotic agents

C(h)loral preparations – chloral hydrate cloral betaine and triclofos

These products are irritant to the stomach, toxic in overdose and interact with alcohol, leading to dangerous respiratory depression.

Clomethiazole

A short-acting compound that can sometimes be useful in the elderly because levels do not accumulate. Toxic in overdose, it interacts similarly with alcohol and readily produces dependence. The liquid preparation is particularly foul-tasting and needs to be well diluted with water or fruit juice before swallowing. Because of its irritant nature many patients sneeze with their first dose (the mustard effect).

Melatonin

June 2008 saw the launch of the first licensed melatonin product (Circadin) for primary insomnia in the over-55 age group. As a 2mg tablet with a 3-week limit on continuous use, its launch only goes part way to meeting the wider use and needs for melatonin products. Many clients' needs (e.g. children and those requiring more than 2mg at night) will sit outside of this licensed framework and this is already recognised by the licensing governing body (MHRA). The view of the MHRA is that this product should be used wherever possible and other formulations sought only when the physical presentation (i.e. a 2mg solid-dose tablet) is a barrier to administration.

For clients who need a liquid presentation or a 2mg capsule – to enable contents to be added to food – these forms will need to continue to be imported from abroad. Under these circumstances the MHRA requires written confirmation from the clinician to be provided in support of the prescription before the pharmacy can proceed with the importation of the alternative melatonin product.

The 'Z' drugs

Zopiclone   (Zimovane)

Zolpidem   (Stilnoct)

Zaleplon   (Sonata)

These three sleeping (hypnotic) agents do not have the additional broad spectrum of activity of the benzodiazepines, with zolpidem and zaleplon binding only to a small portion of the benzodiazepine receptor complex. Zaleplon has the shortest half-life and is indicated for more immediate relief of insomnia. It should not be used for longer than two weeks continuous treatment. Zopiclone and zolpidem may be used on a regular basis for up to four weeks. All three agents are generally well tolerated although zopiclone has been associated with a bitter metallic taste as a frequent side effect and reports of withdrawal reactions following cessation of treatment.

NICE regards them all as essentially identical and recommends using the cheapest and not switching between agents other than for tolerability difficulties. In clinical practice agendas surrounding sedative/hypnotics are often complex and subject to multiple competing influences.

Over-the-counter (OTC) products

A number of proprietary preparations are available for self-purchase from pharmacies for help with anxiety/poor sleep. Many are exploiting the sedative side effects of drugs from other areas, e.g. sedative anti-histamines. A number of patients may also seek out herbal products for similar reasons. Reliance on chronic therapy from this source should be discouraged and it is always useful to ask patients if they are taking any self-selected medicines and record the details.

Other anxiolytics

Buspirone   (Buspar)

This is a specific drug for the treatment of generalised anxiety disorders much more popular in the USA. It differs in several important ways from the benzodiazepines, and will *not* provide direct cover for benzodiazepine withdrawal symptoms.

It does not work quickly and so PRN use is not appropriate. Like anti-depressants it takes 4–6 weeks to give maximum benefit and usually high doses are needed (up to 45 mg daily). For patients who need medication to help with chronic anxiety buspirone may be prone to less tolerance and dependence but currently in the UK short-term use is still specified.

Substance misuse

Dual diagnosis is now an aspect of a significant number of patient presentations. In its literal interpretation the term describes the presence of more than one mental health problem. In reality the label dual diagnosis is taken to refer to a co-morbid substance misuse.

A detailed review of substance misuse in relation to street drugs is beyond the scope of this introduction guide, but it is appropriate to look briefly at issues around smoking cessation, alcohol misuse and opiates (heroin).

Smoking cessation

When patients stop smoking some drug levels can increase. This is because the hydrocarbons in smoke act as inducers of drug-metabolising enzymes. In mental health the most significant effect of stopping smoking and increased drug levels lies with the anti-psychotic clozapine. Levels of clozapine in someone who stops smoking may increase by up to 50 per cent. A dose reduction is likely to be needed and close observation for return of early side effects.

For those genuinely wishing to quit smoking and wanting a pharmacological agent to help them then nicotine replacement therapy (NRT) represents the first-line treatment. NRT is available in many forms (e.g. patches, gum, lozenges) and the patient's preference should be respected. NRT is introduced in tandem with ceasing smoking and limited treatment is supported by the NHS, although products are available to purchase over the counter from local pharmacies.

Varenicline (Champix) is the most recent addition and acts as a partial stimulant (agonist) at the nicotine receptors, providing enough stimulation to avert withdrawal effects but less than a full nicotine reward. It is commenced some days before smoking is stopped, and in order to minimise early nausea there is a 1-week titration to full dose. A course of treatment lasts 12 weeks. It is currently the most expensive agent on the market but is considered a cost-effective alternative to nicotine replacement therapy (NRT).

Bupropion (Zyban) has been available in the USA for some years as an anti-depressant but can only be prescribed in the UK as part of a smoking cessation intervention. It is a non-nicotine pharmacological option to NRT but carries a risk of inducing seizures in vulnerable patients. It is prescribed as a discrete 6–8 week course starting a few days before smoking is stopped. It acts by breaking the craving and reward aspects that prompt smoking activity.

Alcohol and psychotropic medication

Many patients on long-term psychotropics will ask at some point 'Can I drink with these tablets?' For most patients an occasional social drink will be fine although it should be stressed that some additional sleepiness/sedation may be felt. This is more likely early on in therapy and more pronounced with already sedative agents (e.g. tricyclic anti-depressants such as amitriptyline). In these circumstances special care should be taken regarding driving and operating machines where alertness and good concentration are paramount.

To prevent alcohol problems arising men should not drink more than 21 units per week and women 14 units; this allocation should be spread out over the week with occasional alcohol-free days.

Chronic alcohol misuse can lead to liver damage, peptic ulcer, vitamin deficiency (principally water soluble B group) and neurological damage. Management of acute withdrawal reactions ('DTs' and protection against seizures) involves high-dose benzodiazepine such as chlordiazepoxide or diazepam over a 10–14 day reducing schedule and neurological assessment. If there are markers of alcohol neuropathology (e.g. opthalmoplegia) high-dose parenteral thiamine in the form of Pabrinex must be prescribed. A wider nutritional assessment including full blood count may be helpful in identifying any other necessary supplements such as folate or iron and help determine the length of maintenance dosing of oral thiamine and B vitamins. It is very important to note that oral thiamine in any dose will never replace severely depleted brain thiamine stores.

Disulfiram and acamprosate (*BNF* section 4.10)

These agents are used to help with relapse prevention but from two very different angles.

Disulfiram (Antabuse) is taken once daily and provides the patient with an unpleasant reaction if alcohol is taken alongside. The drug blocks the normal pathway of elimination of alcohol allowing levels of an intermediate compound called acetaldehyde to build up. The unpleasant effects provoked by acetaldehyde include facial flushing, increased heart rate, headache, nausea and dizziness with a likely marked drop in blood pressure. Reactions may occasionally be more serious and the practice of 'alcohol challenge' is no longer recommended.

Patients on disulfiram must be warned to keep away from non-drink sources of alcohol such as sprays and lotions and certain foods like spirit vinegar as these may provoke an unpleasant reaction.

Acamprosate (Campral EC) suppresses the craving for alcohol. Taken at a dose of *two tablets three times a day* it causes few side effects and no interaction with alcohol. Coupled with a high degree of motivation to stay off alcohol and engagement with the resource material provided by (but independent of) the company this drug can be very helpful for some individuals.

Both disulfiram and acamprosate taken together may be employed for some patients but all pharmacological treatment for relapse prevention should be thoroughly reviewed after one year.

Opiate substitution

Methadone and buprenorphine (Subutex/Suboxone) represent licensed products that are used to replace and stabilise chaotic and dangerous use of street-based heroin. Methadone is most often prescribed in liquid form and early into treatment patients may take their daily doses under supervision at the local pharmacy. A sugar-free preparation with a simple formulation is best. In drug-naive patients and children methadone can be dangerous so prescribing and monitoring regimens are very much driven by individual risk assessments. It is important to prescribe an adequate dose to manage withdrawal otherwise the patient is likely to source street alternatives to control unmet needs. Buprenorphine is administered by the sub-lingual route (under the tongue); if swallowed it is inactivated very quickly by the liver. It is much safer in overdose than methadone because it is a partial agonist rather than a full agonist at opiate receptors. For the same reason there is less euphoria and rush with this substitute agent although it is still a 'controlled drug' and subject to misuse especially by injection as it is more water soluble.

Methadone and buprenorphine may continue long term with the value of stabilising a patient and reducing criminal acts to source a drug habit or as a 'stepping stone' to an ultimate exit from this type of drug misuse.

Buprenorphine is also available combined with naloxone in the proprietary product Suboxone. The presence of naloxone (which is not absorbed from under the tongue) is there to stop any benefit from injection as naloxone blocks the effects of any opiate at its target receptors. However, naloxone is very short acting and in clinical practice there are reports of Suboxone being misused and so it should not be seen as a substitute for a robust supervised consumption programme. While Suboxone will continue with its patent price tag, generic buprenorphine could represent a cheaper formulation of the principal agent.

Chapter 16
Older adults, children, unlicensed drugs

Older adults

In the main older adults require lower doses of psychiatric medicines. This arises for a number of reasons; drug turnover (metabolism) slows with increasing age and pharmacological effects may become exaggerated. As a result of increased sensitivity to a drug's action, side effects may be more problematic. Hence it is not unusual to find lower dosing schedules recommended for the elderly.

Although many of the mental health problems seen in adults will also be observed in the field of old-age psychiatry this client group has virtually unique ownership of dementia.

Dementia is a **syndrome**; it is not a synonym for confusion, and a confused presentation in an elderly person does not automatically mean dementia.

Many factors can contribute to a *pseudo* dementia-like presentation, including pre-existing medical conditions, sensory impairment, infection, medication, substance (alcohol) misuse and abnormal biochemistry.

There is no one clinical test for dementia but rather the diagnosis is achieved as much by exclusion of these other causative factors.

Just as there can be many reasons for a person becoming confused, there are a number of different types and causes of dementia. Figure 16.1 provides further details of the dementia sub-types and clinical presentations.

Dementia	An acquired global impairment of intellect, memory and personality, but without the clouding of consciousness. Impairments of cognitive function are commonly accompanied and occasionally preceded by deterioration in emotional control, social behaviour or motivation.
Confusion	Signs and symptoms which indicate that the patient is unable to think with customary clarity and logic/reasoning.
Delirium	A reversible and fluctuating state of altered consciousness often accompanied by mood changes, abnormal perceptions and cognitive impairment.
Incidence	5–10 per cent in those over 65 years; 20 per cent in those over 80 years.

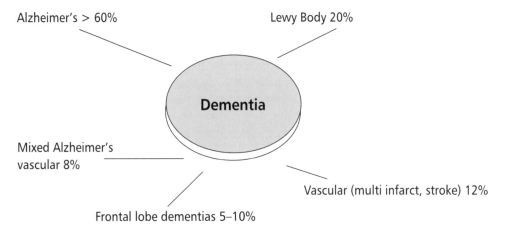

Alzheimer's > 60%

Lewy Body 20%

Dementia

Mixed Alzheimer's vascular 8%

Vascular (multi infarct, stroke) 12%

Frontal lobe dementias 5–10%

Figure 16.1 *Dementia sub-types*

Medications with a specific focus for dementia only slow down the progression of the degenerative process. Such drugs – known as anti-cholinesterases or cholinesterase inhibitors (CHEIs) – increase the action of acetyl-choline, a key brain chemical messenger involved in memory function and known to be reduced in Alzheimer's-type dementia through a number of toxic processes. (See Table 16.1 for some of the side effects.)

Table 16.1 *Cholinesterase side effects*

- Diarrhoea
- Nausea/vomiting
- Insomnia
- Dizziness
- Muscle cramps

CHEIs received endorsement for NHS prescribing in early 2001. This followed guidance issued by NICE and updated in November 2006 (CG number 42). Points to note from the NICE recommendations are as follows:

- While some preliminary differential screening can take place in primary care all patients must be referred to a competent practitioner to establish the diagnosis and initiate treatment. Alzheimer's-type dementia where a Mini Mental State Examination (MMSE) scores between 10 and 20 is endorsed together with unlicensed use in the behavioural management of Lewy Body dementia.

- Attention must be paid to adequate support for compliance with medication.

- The carer's views of the patient's condition form an integral part of the assessment and monitoring process.

- Formal monitoring should include MMSE scoring and measures of global improvement. Initial assessments at approximately one month and three months, then every six months.

- GP prescribing should be carried out under a shared care arrangement.

BNF section 4.11

Donepezil   (Aricept)

Rivastigmine   (Exelon)

Galantamine   (Reminyl)

Memantine (Ebixa)

The first and only treatment licensed for moderate to severe and severe Alzheimer's dementia. It acts on the glutamate receptor complex to prevent cell death when there is advanced neuropathology. Dose titration is from 5 mg daily to 10 mg twice a day over a four-week period. Trials that brought memantine onto the market included patients with a cross-section of dementia sub-types. Statistical differences in a number of domains (e.g. global condition, functional tasks and caregiver burden) *vs* a placebo were identified and the drug is generally well tolerated. In meaningful clinical terms the impact is less impressive and a review by the Scottish Medicines Consortium in 2003 translated these statistical gains into the following clinical conclusion.

> *Compared with placebo it is associated with a statistically significant reduction in the rate of deterioration in global, functional and cognitive scales, but this reduction effectively means a quality of life gain of only six days over a five-year period of continuous treatment. On the evidence presented, the associated gains appear marginal relative to the overall costs.*

Memantine annual costs for maintenance treatment are around £1,000 per patient. NICE 2006 does not support its use in routine clinical practice.

Side effects reported include hallucinations, confusion, dizziness, headache and tiredness.

The drug is available in both tablet and drop formulations.

Management of behavioural and psychological symptoms of dementia (BPSD)

BPSD is a collective term for many of the behaviours (e.g. shouting, pacing, sexual disinhibition) and psychological symptoms (e.g. hallucinations) that occur in patients with dementia.

Using medication from a variety of classes to manage presenting sypmtoms, often anti-psychotics, anxiolytics and other psychotropics are used, based on emerging evidence, anecdotal reports and observed individual outcomes. Atypical anti-psychotics became popular in this regard but in March 2004 attention was drawn by the Committee on the Safety of Medicines (CSM now known as MHRA) to the increased risk of stroke with olanzapine and risperidone. Subsequent evaluations have cast doubt whether other anti-psychotics pose less risk and so any prescription of atypical or alternative agent is best made in a multidisciplinary setting on an individual risk *vs* benefit assessment in collaboration with carers.

To guide clinical decision-making in this difficult area the Royal College of Psychiatrists Faculty for the Psychiatry of Old Age has produced working guidelines at **www.rcpsych.ac.uk/PDF/BPSD.pdf**.

Child and adolescent mental health

Attention deficit disorder (ADD), hyperactive disorders or the more commonly encountered composite ADHD (attention-deficit hyperactivity disorder) is the principal focus for pharmacological strategies within this client group. Alongside behavioural and psychological therapies paradoxically it is stimulant drugs (amphetamines, methylphenidate) that represent the mainstay of pharmacological treatment, although some youngsters respond well to tricyclic anti-depressants (TCAs). An alternative non-stimulant based treatment is atomoxetine (Strattera).

Table 16.2 summarises the key features of ADHD: incidence is estimated at between 6 and 9 per cent based on US data where it continues to be more readily diagnosed.

Table 16.2 *Key features of ADHD*

Inattention	Hyperactivity	Impulsivity
• Easily distracted • Little attention to detail/makes careless mistakes • Does not complete tasks • Difficulty organising activities • Does not seem to listen when directly spoken to	• Fidgets • Acts as if being 'driven by a motor' • Leaves seat at inappropriate times • Difficulty playing quietly • Talks excessively	• Difficulty waiting turn • Intrudes on others • Blurts out answers before question is completed

The cardinal features should be pervasive across situations (e.g. school, home), excessive for age and IQ, persistent over time and severe enough to interfere with social, academic or occupational function.

Co-morbidity with other forms of disruptive behaviour such as conduct or oppositional defiant disorders is common.

ADHD sufferers are often unpopular with other children, tend to become isolated and suffer low self-esteem.

Stimulant medication (*BNF* section 4.4)

Dexamphetamine   (Dexedrine)

Methylphenidate   (Ritalin, Equasym, Equasym XL, Concerta XL)

Stimulants are understood to provide benefit by their action on dopamine and noradrenaline pathways in the cerebral cortex, where they promote an exaggerated release of these transmitters from their nerve endings. Increasing transmitter activity here leads to a reduction in impulsiveness and hyperactivity.

The stimulants are short acting (typically 2–4 hours), necessitating 3–4 doses during the working day. It is important that doses are not given in the evening as the broader stimulant effects are likely to lead to insomnia and bad dreams. Although stimulants are quick to impact, careful titration to optimum dose (typically 30–60 mg methylphenidate per day) is required and a check on blood pressure, weight and general childhood development is needed. Stimulants typically have appetite suppressant properties and chronic use may retard normal growth.

Issues around frequent dosing during the day due to the short half-life of the drug apply equally to both children and adults, where the abrupt wearing off of a dose can prompt dramatic rebound effects.

For children midday dosing can present problems: depending on the school's policy regarding medication the situation is often made more difficult to resolve by awareness of the potential for diversion and misuse. The advent of modified release methylphenidate (Equasym XL and Concerta XL) has helped this situation by allowing a reduced frequency of dosing outside of school hours. Conversion from conventional methylphenidate to Concerta XL is best done under specialist guidance as the doses of the two preparations are not identical.

Atomoxetine (Strattera)

A fairly complex dose titration is required; once daily or twice daily divided dosing is possible.

Atomoxetine is a specific noradrenaline re-uptake inhibitor and differs from the stimulant medications in a number of ways.

- It focuses only on noradrenaline and increases its activity by reducing the re-uptake of physiologically released noradrenaline back into the nerve endings.

- It is not fast acting and full benefit can take 4–6 weeks to fully emerge.

- It is not a controlled drug and is unlikely to be part of any substance misuse agenda as it lacks any direct stimulant or euphoriant properties.

- It is indicated (licensed) for children *but the adult licence was withdrawn in February 2005 pending the gathering of long-term efficacy data to satisfy the wider European market*.

- It does not exacerbate co-morbid mood disorders or tics.

Similar monitoring of blood pressure, weight and general childhood development parameters is advised.

While there would appear to be far less of the short-term adverse effects associated with stimulants some adverse effects overlap, principally insomnia and loss of appetite. Gastrointestinal upset is frequently reported.

Atomoxetine can be safely cross-tapered with stimulant medication.

Cautions regarding rare but serious liver toxicity, risk of seizures and monitoring for signs of suicidality have been issued more recently.

ADHD in adults

For many years ADHD was regarded as a condition which resolved on reaching adulthood but it is now becoming accepted that around *two-thirds* of children (usually boys) will continue into adulthood with some modified clinical symptoms.

ADHD is only ever diagnosed *prima face* in childhood, usually after school entry age, and retrospective recognition requires strong evidence from school reports and relevant carers.

Adults with untreated ADHD symptoms often attract poor employment records, have more car driving accidents and present with a high degree of co-morbidity including mood disorders, anxiety disorders and personality disorders. Substance misuse is seen in around *half* of cases.

Evidence from clinical trials points towards benefit from the same types of treatment although no medication carries a formal licence for adult use and doses are likely to be higher than those quoted for children.

With regard to stimulants it should be noted that adult days are longer than a child's day and some night-time activities such as driving may require medication cover. If travelling abroad there is a limit on how much controlled drug may be taken abroad before a Home Office licence is required. See **www.hmrc.gov.uk** for more information.

The following resources can provide you with further information:

- your local accredited specialist mental health pharmacist (MCMHP);

- your local Medicines Information department (often part of the hospital pharmacy).

Unlicensed use

All medicinal products on the UK market have listed indications of their use, which is detailed in the summary of product characteristics (SPC) – previously called the data sheet. If the drug is given for a condition not covered by the SPC or the dose is outside of that listed in the SPC then its use in that patient is known as *unlicensed*. (Off-label is another term.)

Under such circumstances the prescriber takes a personal responsibility for the use of the drug in that patient and could be sued personally if any untoward incident arises. In practice the prescriber, if acting reasonably (Bolam test), would be covered by his employer.

Many drug companies do not seek costly licence extensions when there is unlikely to be significant commercial gain although there may be good evidence to support its use in that therapeutic area.

Unlicensed use is not unlawful and should not be presumed as suggesting unsafe practice. However, it should be clearly documented in a patient's notes with the patient fully informed.

Chapter 17
The law and psychiatric treatment

Valid consent in psychiatric treatment

Under English law the principle of informed consent to treatment is not absolute. Indeed, informed consent is an American and Australian concept which does not fully obtain in England and Wales, where the relevant concept is valid consent. There is a general legal requirement that consent to treatment should be based on the patient being informed as to the nature of a proposed treatment, its purposes and any hazards associated with it. This does not mean, however, that the doctor must tell the patient about every conceivable risk attached to the treatment. He or she is only obliged to inform the patient of such risks in broad terms, and the law allows the doctor to exercise professional judgement as to what the patient is told.

The current position on consent was set in a case of a woman who sued a surgeon for failing to inform her fully of the known potential hazard of partial paralysis resulting from an operation to her neck (*Sidaway* vs *Bethlem Royal Hospital*, 1957). In that case it was held that a treating doctor might reasonably exercise professional judgement in deciding how much information should be given to a patient. A doctor may not obtain valid consent by deceiving a patient about the nature or effects of a treatment. Neither may he or she exercise force or duress to obtain such consent. In an emergency a treatment may be given if it is necessary to save a life.

This chapter will provide an overview of the law on consent now that the Mental Capacity Act 2005 is in force. Chapter 18 will look at the particular requirements of the Mental Health Act 1983 when treating patients who are subject to compulsion.

Principles

The Act has five key principles which are set out in section 1.

1 *A person must be assumed to have capacity unless it is established that he lacks capacity.*

2 *A person is not to be treated as unable to make a decision unless all practicable steps to help him to do so have been taken without success.*

3 *A person is not to be treated as unable to make a decision merely because he makes an unwise decision.*

4 *An act done, or decision made, under this Act for or on behalf of a person who lacks capacity must be done, or made, in his best interests.*

5 *Before the act is done, or the decision is made, regard must be had to whether the purpose for which it is needed can be as effectively achieved in a way that is less restrictive of the person's rights and freedom of action.*

The starting position for any medical treatment is therefore that the person, if aged 16 or more, is presumed to have capacity and may therefore accept or reject any offer of treatment whether for physical or mental disorder. The exceptions provided for those subject to compulsion under the Mental Health Act are considered separately in the following chapter. So if a patient has capacity they decide whether to accept treatment. How does the mental health professional decide whether or not the person has capacity?

Defining who lacks capacity

This is set out in section 2 of the Mental Capacity Act:

For the purposes of this Act, a person lacks capacity in relation to a matter if at the material time he is unable to make a decision for himself in relation to the matter because of an impairment of, or a disturbance in the functioning of, the mind or brain. It does not matter whether the impairment or disturbance is permanent or temporary.

The issue of capacity is therefore instant-specific. Let us consider the situation where a doctor is proposing a particular treatment for an informal patient. Section 3(2) states that:

A person is not to be regarded as unable to understand the information relevant to a decision if he is able to understand an explanation of it given to him in a way that is appropriate to his circumstances (using simple language, visual aids or any other means).

This is sometimes referred to as the diagnostic test. Its breadth is effectively cut down by application of the functional test, i.e. only the precise area of decision-making necessary is identified for application of the incapacity test.

Section 3 of the Mental Capacity Act then sets out the test that should be used. It is a development of tests that had been established by the courts in cases such as that of the man with the gangrenous leg (C *[Adult: Refusal of Medical Treatment]*, 1994).

The section 3 test is that:

[A] person is unable to make a decision for himself if he is unable:

(a) *to understand the information relevant to the decision,*

(b) *to retain that information,*

(c) *to use or weigh that information as part of the process of making the decision, or*

(d) *to communicate his decision (whether by talking, using sign language or any other means).*

In relation to a proposed course of treatment, an inability to satisfy any one of these four conditions would render the person incapable. In proceedings under this Act any question of whether a person lacks capacity must be decided on the balance of probabilities.

Memory requirement

The fact that a person is able to retain the information relevant to a decision for a short period only does not prevent them from being regarded as being able to make the decision. The information relevant to a decision includes information about reasonably foreseeable consequences of deciding one way or another or failing to make the decision. This means that the length of time a person would need to remember the information would depend on the complexity of the procedure. A simple procedure, however serious, might still be within the capacity of someone with memory problems to make the decision. They would need to remember the information only long enough to complete the process of weighing it in the balance, making the decision and communicating this.

If a person has capacity, not only can they make a current decision about treatment; there are two further ways that the Mental Capacity Act helps them to stay in control of their own medical affairs.

Advance decisions to refuse treatment

If a person is aged 18 or over, and has capacity, they can decide that a specified treatment should not be carried out or continued if:

• at a later time in specified circumstances the treatment is proposed;

• at that time they lack capacity to consent.

Advance decisions will not be valid if a person withdraws when capable or has subsequently created lasting power of attorney conferring on the donee power to make decisions on the treatment in question. They will also be invalid if the person has done anything else clearly inconsistent with the advance decision.

Where it addresses life-sustaining treatment the advance directive should be in writing and should be witnessed. For other treatments there is no such requirement. However, the refusal needs to be seen as valid and applicable in the particular circumstances which present themselves and, for this reason, recording a decision is to be advised in most cases.

Lasting powers of attorney (LPA)

The second method of retaining more control is to make a lasting power of attorney. A donor can confer authority to take decisions about personal welfare or property and affairs (or specified matters within these areas) subject to certain requirements.

This power of attorney can be made jointly or severally (if not specified it will be assumed to be jointly). Again the person with power of attorney cannot restrain the donor unless they lack, or the donee reasonably believes that they lack, capacity in relation to the matter in question. The donee (sometimes referred to as the attorney) must reasonably believe that it is necessary to do the act in order to prevent harm to the person and that the act is a proportionate response to the likelihood of their suffering harm, and to the seriousness of that harm. This new LPA is potentially very important in the mental health field. Once it has been registered, doctors will need to obtain consent from the donee.

Incapacity and best interests

Before the implementation of the Mental Capacity Act, the common law already recognised the 'doctrine of necessity' which applied to anyone intervening for someone who lacked capacity in relation to a decision. This principle found its way into statute with the new Act in section 1(5) as identified above. The key elements of operating the best interests principle are set out in section 4.

- A person acting for someone else must consider all relevant circumstances in deciding what is in the other person's best interests.

- Regard must be had as to whether or when the person is likely to regain capacity.

- A person should be encouraged to participate in the decision as fully as possible.

- Past and present wishes and feelings should be considered (and, in particular, any relevant written statement made by the person when they had capacity).

- Consideration should be given to beliefs and values which would have been likely to influence their decision if they had capacity, and to the other factors that they would have been likely to consider if they were able to do so.

- The acting person must consult, if practicable, anyone named by the incapacitated person, anyone caring for them or interested in their welfare, any donee or deputy, as to what would be in their best interests.

These points are not mere guidance. They are in the Act itself and so must be followed to justify any intervention based on lack of capacity.

Section 5 requires that D (the person acting) for a person (P) must take reasonable steps to establish whether P lacks capacity in relation to the matter in question and, at the time of acting, believes that P lacks capacity and that the act is in their best interests.

D cannot restrain P (i.e. use force, the threat of force or restrict movement) unless it is necessary to prevent harm to P and it is proportionate to the likelihood and seriousness of the harm. This means that in practice a significant amount of treatment for mental disorder is given under this provision although the authors have some concern about professional awareness of this and about the quality of recording in this area.

Deprivation of liberty

There has been an alteration in the wording of the Mental Capacity Act now that the Deprivation of Liberty Safeguards (DOLS) are in place.

Sections 4A and 4B state that the Act only authorises a person to deprive another of their liberty where this is linked to:

- a Court of Protection order under section 16;

- an authorisation under the new DOLS procedure;

- where a decision is awaited from the court and the person is to be given life-sustaining treatment or a vital act is to be preformed.

A vital act is defined as *any act which the person doing it reasonably believes to be necessary to prevent a serious deterioration in P's condition*.

Where a patient is in hospital and the treatment is so invasive that it amounts to the factor that tips the patient over the dividing line from 'restriction of movement' to 'deprivation of liberty' it seems to the authors to be likely that a doctor will wish to consider the use of the Mental Health Act (see next chapter). In some cases in care homes a deprivation of liberty may necessitate use of the new DOLS procedure (especially if guardianship is not considered to meet the needs). For a fuller discussion of this area of law see Brown, Barber and Martin (2009).

The Court of Protection

The reformed Court of Protection is central to many parts of the new Act. The Court has powers to decide whether a person has or lacks capacity to make a decision. The Court is able to determine the lawfulness of acts, omissions or the course of conduct relating to a person. In some case the Court might decide to appoint a 'deputy' to make decisions on P's behalf. However, it is expected that in most cases the Court will make a single order about a matter. At the time of writing the court has been under pressure and there is a considerable backlog of work. It has already been criticised for being cumbersome, expensive and unresponsive to the difficulties faced by practitioners. The procedures for lasting powers of attorney are being streamlined and made less expensive. More work is needed on the Court of Protection if it is to be regarded positively by practitioners.

The gateway to the Court of Protection is the Public Guardian, who:

- keeps a register of lasting powers of attorney;

- keeps a register of orders appointing deputies;

- supervises donees of lasting powers of attorney and deputies;

- directs visits (by Court of Protection visitors).

There are some excellent guidance notes and leaflets available by accessing the Office's website on: **www.publicguardian.gov.uk**. This is also the easiest way of keeping up to date with the operation of the Mental Capacity Act.

Children

The Family Law Reform Act 1969 states that the presumption of capacity starts at the age of 16 so in terms of agreeing to treatment a young person over the age of 16 has the same rights in consent procedures as an adult. This position was reinforced by the introduction of the Mental Capacity Act.

Under the age of 16 the Gillick case applies and if the child is able to understand the relevant information and weigh it in the balance, etc. (in much the same way as in the MCA) they will be able to give consent to treatment. Until recently the position was, somewhat perversely, that they could not effectively refuse treatment until the age of 18 as a doctor could rely on parental consent until that age. However, the reforms of the Mental Capacity Act 2007 mean that, at least for the purposes of admission and treatment in a psychiatric hospital, this is no longer the case.

General treatment issues

There are a number if issues which a psychiatrist will bear in mind when deciding on a treatment plan.

The severity of the symptoms

These can be very distressing to the patient and those around them. The distress felt by the patient must be the first consideration, with that of relatives or others second. This is not to say the distress of relatives or others is unimportant; rather, that those involved in giving treatment must be clear as to whose distress or anxieties are being dealt with. It is not acceptable to pressure a patient into taking a drug or a higher dose of a drug simply for the convenience of others. The distress experienced by a patient as a result of a drug's effects may far exceed any embarrassment or inconvenience caused to others.

The strain imposed on those caring for the patient

Serious mental illness can cause people to behave in disturbed, disruptive and occasionally dangerous ways. It may be necessary to protect families from intolerable strains imposed by such behaviour in order to protect that patient's place within the family.

The risk of leaving dangerous symptoms untreated

In some instances it is necessary to give treatment in order to safeguard the safety of the patient, as well as other people. If the patient has capacity this presents an ethical and legal dilemma if the patient refuses the treatment.

The benefits of the treatment versus the disadvantages

As will be seen in this guide, the drugs used in psychiatry are not effective for all patients, and some of the drugs expose patients to risks without any realistic expectations of benefits being gained. For some patients the treatment may be worse than the illness, while for others the risks and side effects of the drugs may be a small price to pay for the relief they bring from tormenting or dangerous symptoms. The strategy of steadily increasing the doses of anti-psychotic drugs when they have been shown to be ineffective is dangerous and unacceptable. There are situations in which physical restraint is more acceptable than attempts to stun people with powerful drugs.

Consent and mental health law

A small (but increasing) proportion of people receiving treatment for mental disorder are detained under the 1983 Mental Health Act. The minority who are liable to be detained may in certain circumstances be administered treatment without their consent. The position of patients subject to detention is set out in the next chapter. All patients with capacity who are not subject to detention in hospital under the provisions of the Mental Health Act can refuse any treatment which they would rather not have. They have the same rights as anyone else to give or withhold valid consent, and in theory they should give such consent before they are given any treatment. In practice however, it may be that they are neither asked for consent nor informed of their rights. Medication may be treated simply as a matter of routine. There are competing views on this issue. One view is that, in psychiatry, if the law on consent to treatment was observed to the letter, considerable inconvenience would be caused to those who prescribe and administer treatments. However, there is a competing view that more formal consent procedures might do much to improve the quality of treatment and the quality of relationships between patients and staff, which could ultimately lead to patients complying with treatment more readily.

Conclusion. The principle components of valid consent

Information

The patient must be given information on the nature and purpose of the treatment and any serious side effects or hazards (the doctor is not obliged to inform the patient of every possible side effect or hazard but must not deceive the patient).

Competence

The patient must be able to understand the nature and purpose of the treatment. The fact that someone is suffering from a mental disorder does not automatically mean that they are incapable of understanding the issues involved, but obviously some people will be better able to understand than others.

Voluntariness

The patient must give consent without undue force, persuasion or influence being brought to bear. A consent obtained by fraud, deceit or threat is not legally valid and any person administering treatment under such circumstances would be acting unlawfully.

The only circumstances in which a person not subject to detention under the Mental Health Act can be treated without a consent first being obtained are in circumstances of urgent necessity. For example, it would be lawful in an emergency to give a person suffering from mental illness immediate treatment in order to prevent that person from harming themselves or other people. However, such treatment can only be given for as long as it is necessary to bring the emergency to an end; the patient's consent must be obtained to continue treatment beyond that point.

Chapter 18

Treatment under the Mental Health Act

Introduction

Part 4 of the Mental Health Act has not been fully understood by many practitioners. For example, there is a widespread false belief that patients detained for up to 28 days under section 2 cannot be treated without their consent. In reality there is no difference between sections 2 and 3 when it comes to the legal position on treatment; both are specifically covered by Part 4 because of the provisions of section 56. The introduction of Part 4A to cover patients subject to the new Community Treatment Order, together with some changes to the law on ECT, have complicated matters further. This chapter attempts to make this complex position understandable to practitioners. For a fuller discussion of some of the issues see Barber, Brown and Martin (2009).

As we have seen in the previous chapter, patients not covered by Part 4 or 4A are entitled to refuse or to consent to treatment in the same way as any patient receiving treatment for a physical condition. We also noted that where a patient lacks capacity in relation to the treatment, the Mental Capacity Act may apply.

Barber, Brown and Barber (2009, p55) identified that until the Mental Health Amendment Act which was implemented in 1982:

> there were no special rules for treating detained patients. The approach adopted in 1982 (and consolidated in the 1983 Act) was based on the idea that some patients who are liable to be detained may need treatment without their consent. Certain procedures should be followed to offer safeguards. What may be seen as particularly controversial by many patients is that s63 allows for a vast array of treatments (including medication for the first three months of detention) to be given without the valid consent of the patient. This can even apply where the patient has capacity with regard to the treatment and where they are no risk to anyone else.

Patients covered by Parts 4 and 4A

As a general rule those patients liable to detention for periods of more than 72 hours are covered by Part 4. The one exception is patients who have been remanded for reports by a court under section 35. So patients subject to detention under sections 2, 3 and 37 are covered by Part 4. Patients on Community Treatment Orders (CTOs) are subject to Part 4A unless they are recalled to hospital, in which case they are covered by Part 4 during the period of recall. Guardianship patients are not covered by any special consent to treatment rules. The safeguards for detained patients were altered by the recent amendments, but still involve a second medical opinion from outside the hospital for more serious forms of treatment in those cases where valid consent cannot be obtained from the patient. This lack of consent could either be the result of the patient objecting to the treatment, or of their being unable to give valid consent because they lack mental capacity. For the most serious treatments (such as psychosurgery), a second opinion and the valid consent of the patient are required and these safeguards are extended to informal patients. The Care Quality Commission (CQC) has a duty to oversee the operation of these parts of the Act.

What is medical treatment?

Section 145 of the amended MHA gives a definition of medical treatment as:

> *nursing, psychological intervention and specialist mental health habilitation, rehabilitation and care … the purpose of which is to alleviate, or prevent a worsening of, the disorder or one or more of its symptoms or manifestations.*

It can be seen that this a very broad definition and only certain forms of treatment are covered by special rules. Sections 57, 58 and 58A set out the categories of medical treatment which are covered by separate procedures. Some treatments require the approval of a Second Opinion Appointed Doctor (SOAD) who has been appointed for this purpose. The categories of treatment which are specified in the Act or Regulations are as follows:

> Section 57: any surgical operation for destroying brain tissue or for destroying the functioning of brain tissue (generally known as neurosurgery); or surgical implantation of hormones to reduce male sex drive.

> Section 58: psychiatric medication after three months of treatment while detained.

> Section 58A: electro-convulsive therapy (ECT) and related medication.

The safeguards are set out in more detail below. It is possible in future that other forms of treatment may be added to this list by regulations.

Approved Clinicians

Some treatments can only be given under the direction of an Approved Clinician. Until 2008 medical treatment was given under the direction of a registered medical practitioner but this is no longer a requirement. Instead there are new safeguards covering who can be in charge of certain treatments. For a detained patient the person in charge of the treatment must be registered as an Approved Clinician in the situations where:

- treatment is given without the patient's consent;
- the patient has consented under s58 or 58A and the certificate has been completed by an Approved Clinician rather than a SOAD;

- – a CTO patient has been recalled or the CTO revoked, and
  - – where the s58 requirements have not yet been met but
  - – there is consent and the treatment is necessary to prevent serious suffering to the patient.

For a community patient (i.e. someone subject to a CTO) there needs to be an approved clinician in charge of the treatment being given to a patient where they lack capacity to consent to the treatment unless there is the consent of an attorney (from an LPA), from a deputy or from the Court of Protection itself. Section 64G allows for some exceptions in emergencies.

Part 4 in detail

The forms referred to here are the numbers as per the English Regulations. The Welsh equivalents have different numbers.

Section 57 covers any surgical operation for destroying brain tissue or for destroying the functioning of brain tissue (this is generally referred to as neurosurgery), as well as the surgical implantation of hormones to reduce male sex drive. The safeguards cover informal as well as detained patients. This is because the treatments are seen as so invasive. A SOAD and two other persons appointed by the Care Quality Commission need to certify in writing on form T1 that the patient is capable of understanding the nature, purpose and likely effects of the treatment in question and has consented to it. In addition the SOAD has to certify in writing that it is appropriate for the treatment to be given, having consulted two other persons who have been professionally concerned with the patient's medical treatment. One of these consultees needs to be a nurse and the other should be someone other than a nurse or a doctor. They should record their own views in the medical notes.

It is worth noting that there are usually only three or four cases of neurosurgery under s57 per year in the whole of England and Wales. There have been no s57 referrals for the last 20 years for the surgical implantation of hormones to reduce male sex drive.

Section 58 deals with medication for mental disorder after three months of treatment under detention. It does not cover medication administered as part of ECT treatment as this, along with ECT itself, is covered by s58A. The safeguards under s58 are that medication cannot be given unless:

- the patient has consented to the treatment and either the approved clinician in charge of it, or a SOAD, has certified in writing on form T2 that the patient is capable of understanding its nature, purpose and likely effects and has consented to it; or

- a SOAD has certified in writing on form T3 that the patient is not capable of understanding the nature, purpose and likely effects of that treatment, or is capable but has not consented to it, and that it is appropriate for the treatment to be given. The SOAD must have consulted two other persons who have been professionally concerned with the patient's medical treatment. One of these must be a nurse and the other shall be neither a nurse nor a registered medical practitioner; and neither can be the approved clinician or the person in charge of the treatment in question.

Where treatment is based on a form T2, the Code of Practice recommends that there should be a record in the patient's notes of the relevant discussion where capacity was confirmed and full details of the specific treatment covered. Paragraph 24.17 states:

Certificates under this section must clearly set out the specific forms of treatment to which they apply. All the relevant drugs should be listed, including medication to be given 'as required' (prn), either by name or by the classes described in the British National Formulary (BNF). *If drugs are specified by class, the certificate should state clearly the number of drugs authorised in each class, and whether any drugs within the class are excluded. The maximum dosage and route of administration should be clearly indicated for each drug or category of drugs proposed. This can exceed the dosages listed in the* BNF, *but particular care is required in these cases.*

Section 58A covers ECT and any medication administered as part of the ECT process. As well as adult detained patients, s58A also applies to all patients under the age of 18, whether detained or not. This new section is the first occasion where the Mental Health Act does not take preference over the Mental Capacity Act. If a patient makes a competent refusal or a valid and applicable advance decision, this will prevent treatment from being given under s58A. ECT may not be given to an adult unless one of the following conditions applies.

- They have consented to that treatment and either the approved clinician in charge of it, or a SOAD, has certified on form T4 that the patient is capable of understanding its nature, purpose and likely effects and has consented to it.

- A SOAD has certified on form T6 that the patient is not capable of understanding the nature, purpose and likely effects of the treatment, and that it is appropriate for the treatment to be given, and that this will not conflict with a valid and applicable advance decision or a decision made by a donee or a deputy or the Court of Protection. The SOAD must have consulted two other persons who have been professionally concerned with the patient's medical treatment. One of these must be a nurse and the other shall be neither a nurse nor a registered medical practitioner. Neither of them can be the approved clinician or the person in charge of the treatment in question.

For someone under 18 a certificate from a SOAD is needed both for patients who have capacity and have consented (formT5) or for those who lack capacity (form T6). The certificate by itself is not sufficient authority to treat. The clinician must also have the patient's own consent or some other legal authority at the time of giving the treatment.

Section 62 deals with urgent treatment. In cases of emergency, such as where a patient withdraws consent in the middle of a course of treatment, it allows treatment which is immediately necessary to save the patient's life, or which (not being irreversible) is immediately necessary to prevent a serious deterioration of his condition. It also allows treatment with medication which (not being irreversible or hazardous) is immediately necessary to alleviate serious suffering by the patient; or which (not being irreversible or hazardous) is immediately necessary and represents the minimum interference necessary to prevent the patient from behaving violently or being a danger to himself or to others. Treatment is irreversible if it has *unfavourable irreversible physical or psychological consequences* and hazardous if it entails *significant physical hazard*.

The Regulations do not prescribe a form for s62 but the Code of Practice states at para. 24.37:

> *Hospital managers should monitor the use of these exceptions to the certificate requirements to ensure that they are not used inappropriately or excessively. They are advised to provide a form (or other method) by which the clinician in charge of the treatment in question can record details of:*
>
> - *the proposed treatment;*
> - *why it is immediately necessary to give the treatment; and*
> - *the length of time for which the treatment is given.*

Section 63 covers treatment not requiring consent as long as the treatment is given by or under the direction of the approved clinician in charge of the treatment. This is a major worry for many patients because it means that, apart from ECT, any treatment can be given to a patient in the first three months of their detention without their valid consent. After three months the safeguard of the SOAD's involvement applies but even this is only in relation to medication. Many other treatments (e.g. psychological) can continue to be given without any involvement of a SOAD. Human rights challenges may be anticipated.

Table 18.1 Consent to treatment flowchart for Part 4

Adapted from *Mental Health Law: A Practice Guide* by Puri, B. et al. (2005)

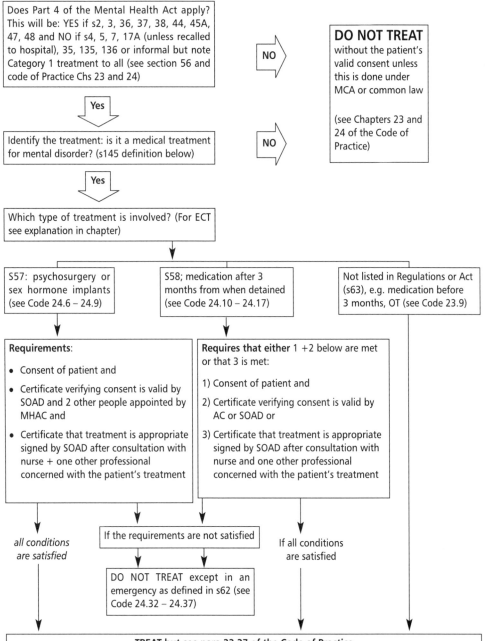

Note: 'medical treatment' is defined in section 145 as including *nursing, psychological intervention and specialist mental health habilitation, rehabilitation and care ... the purpose of which is to alleviate, or prevent a worsening of, the disorder or one or more of its symptoms or manifestations.*

Part 4A – Treatment of community patients

This new part of the Act provides safeguards for the treatment for patients who are subject to CTOs (and where they have not been recalled). A CTO patient cannot be given treatment for mental disorder unless the requirements of Part 4A are met. This means that the person giving the treatment must have the authority to do so, and in most cases there will be a certification requirement. Form CTO11 is needed for treatments which would have required a certificate under s58 or 58A if the patient were still detained. In effect this means medication after the initial three-month period and ECT (and any related medication) at any time. A certificate is not required during the first month of a patient's discharge from detention on to a CTO even if the three-month period for s58 has already expired or expires during this first month.

When deciding whether to issue a certificate the SOAD does not have to certify whether a patient has, or lacks, capacity to consent to the treatment. Similarly they do not have to judge whether a patient with capacity is consenting or refusing. Their function is to decide whether the treatment is appropriate for the patient. They may make it a condition of their approval that particular treatments are given only in certain circumstances. The Code of Practice gives examples at para. 24.27:

> they might specify that a particular treatment is to be given only with the patient's consent. Similarly, they might specify that a medication may be given up to a certain dosage if the patient lacks capacity to consent, but that a higher dosage may be given with the patient's consent.

SOADs need to consider the possibility that the patient could be recalled to hospital with a view to giving them treatment. The SOAD can decide which treatments to approve in the event of the patient being recalled to hospital and whether to impose any conditions on that approval. Unless it states otherwise, the certificate will authorise the treatment even if the patient has capacity to refuse it. The SOAD must consult two other people who have been professionally concerned with the patient's medical treatment. Only one of these may be a doctor and neither of them can be the patient's approved clinician or the approved clinician in charge of any of the treatments that are to be specified on the certificate.

Authority to treat

Where a patient over the age of 16 has capacity to consent to treatment, this is what provides the authority to treat. In some cases there may be a an attorney under an LPA, or a deputy appointed by the Court of Protection. This person may be able to consent on the patient's behalf depending on the LPA or level of authority given to the deputy.

Where the CTO patient lacks capacity to consent to the treatment, the person wishing to have the authority to treat must take reasonable steps to establish that the patient lacks capacity to consent to the treatment. Then, when giving the treatment, he must reasonably believe that the patient lacks capacity to consent to it and:

- have no reason to believe that the patient objects to being given the treatment; or, if he does have reason to believe that the patient objects, it is not necessary to use force against the patient in order to give the treatment;

- be the person in charge of the treatment and an approved clinician; or the treatment must be given under the direction of that clinician;

- ensure that giving the treatment will not conflict with an advance decision which he is satisfied is valid and applicable, or with a decision made by a donee or deputy or the Court of Protection.

Emergencies

If treatment is to be given without a certificate, the treatment must fall into one of the following categories set out in section 64G(5):

(a) *it is immediately necessary to save the patient's life; or*

(b) *it is immediately necessary to prevent a serious deterioration of the patient's condition and is not irreversible; or*

(c) *it is immediately necessary to alleviate serious suffering by the patient and is not irreversible or hazardous; or*

(d) *it is immediately necessary, represents the minimum interference necessary to prevent the patient from behaving violently or being a danger to himself or others and is not irreversible or hazardous.*

Somewhat controversially this provision had to be used in the first few months of the CTO being introduced because the numbers of CTOs were so high that the SOAD system was overstretched.

Sample question from AMHP paper on consent to treatment and mental capacity

1a *What is an advance decision and how might this relate to psychiatric medication?*

1b *What issues may arise if someone makes an advance decision in relation to the use of a particular anti-psychotic drug and is later admitted to psychiatric hospital under section 2?*

1c *What difficulties might an AMHP face in these circumstances (before and after admission)?*

Statutes

1938 Infanticide Act

1964 Criminal Procedures (Insanity) Act (as amended in 1991)

1969 Family Law Reform Act

1976 and 2000 Race Relations Acts

1977 National Health Service Act

1983 Mental Health Act

1984 Police and Criminal Evidence Act

1989 Children Act

1990 National Health Service and Community Care Act

1998 Human Rights Act

1999 Health Act

2005 Mental Capacity Act

2007 Mental Health Act

Case law

Bolam v *Friern Hospital* [1957] IWRL 582

C (*Adult: Refusal of Medical Treatment*), Re [1994] 1WLR 290

Gillick v *West Norfolk and Wisbech Area Health Authority and Another* [1986] AC112

HL v *UK* [2004] 40 EHRR 761, [2004] 1 FLR 1019

McNaghten's Case [1843] 10 CI&F 200

R (*on the application of von Brandenburg*) v *East London and City Mental Health NHS Trust* [2004] 1 All ER 400

Sidaway v *Bethlem Royal Hospital* [1985] AC871

Some useful websites

British National Formulary	**www.bnf.org/bnf**
Care Quality Commission	**www.cqc.org.uk**
Department of Health	**www.dh.gov.uk**
Healthcare Inspectorate Wales	**www.hiw.org.uk**
Mental health law (IMHAP members site)	**www.imhap.org.uk**
Ministry of Justice	**www.justice.gov.uk**
Public Guardian	**www.publicguardian.gov.uk**
Royal College of Psychiatrists	**www.rcpsych.ac.uk/college**

References

American Psychiatric Association (1994) *Diagnostic and Statistical Manual of Mental Disorders*. APA.

Barber, P., Brown, R. and Martin, D. (2009) Mental Health Law in England and Wales. Learning Matters.

Bowlby, J. (1969) *Attachment* [Vol. 1 of *Attachment and Loss*]. Hogarth Press.

Bowlby, J. (1973) *Separation: Anxiety & Anger* [Vol. 2 of *Attachment and Loss*]. Hogarth Press.

British National Formulary (2009) *BNF Volume 57*. BNF.

Brown, R. (2009) *The Approved Mental Health Professional's Guide to Mental Health Law*. Learning Matters.

Brown, R., Barber, P. and Martin, D. *(2009). The Mental Capacity Act 2005.* Learning Matters.

CCETSW (2000) *Assuring Quality for Mental Health Social Work*. CCETSW.

Craig, M. (2004) 'Perinatal risk factors for neonaticide and infant homicide: can we identify those at risk?', *Journal of the Royal Society of Medicine*, 97: 57–61.

Department of Health (2007) *Explanatory Notes to the Mental Health Act 2007*. TSO.

Department of Health (2008a) *Mental Health Act 1983. Code of Practice.* TSO.

Department of Health (2008b) *Mental Health Act 1983. Reference Guide.* TSO.

Department of Health and Home Office (1992) *Review of Mental Health and Social Services for Mentally Disordered Offenders and Others Requiring Similar Services: Vol. 1: Final Summary Report* [The Reed Report], Cm. 2088. HMSO.

D'Orban, P. T. (1979) 'Women who kill their children', *British Journal of Psychiatry*, 134: 560–71.

Falkov, A. (1996) *A Study of Working Together. 'Part 8 Reports': Fatal Child Abuse and Parental Psychiatric Disorder*. Department of Health.

Fraiberg, S., Adelson, E. and Shapiro, V. (1980) Ghosts in the nursery: a psychoanalytic approach to the problems of impaired infant–mother relationships', in S. Fraiberg (ed.), *Clinical Studies in Infant Mental Health*. Basic Books, pp. 164–96.

Hare, R. D. (1991) *The Hare Psychopathy Checklist – Revised*. Multi-Health Systems.

Home Office (2008) *Police and Criminal Evidence Act 1984: Codes of Practice*. TSO.

Home Office and Department of Health (1999) *Managing Dangerous People with Severe Personality Disorder*. TSO.

Home Office, Department of Health and the Welsh Office (2007) *Guidance for Social Supervisors*. TSO.

Jones, R. (ed.) (2008) *Mental Health Act Manual*, 11th edn. Sweet & Maxwell.

Law Commission (1991) *Mentally Incapacitated Adults and Decision-Making. An Overview*, Consultation Paper No. 119. HMSO.

Law Commission (1995) *Mentally Incapacity*, LAW COM No. 231.

Melville, H. (1924) *Billy Budd, Sailor*. Penguin.

Montgomery, J. (2009) *Health Care Law*. Oxford University Press.

Murray, L. and Cooper, P. (eds) (1999) *Postpartum Depression and Child Development*. Guilford Press.

Puri, B., Brown, R., McKee, H. and Treasaden, I. (2005) *Mental Health Law*. Hodder Arnold.

Resnick, P. (1970) 'Murder of the newborn: a psychiatric review', *American Journal of Psychiatry*, 126: 1414–20.

Rutter, M., Graham, P. and Yule, W. (1970) A Neuropsychiatric Study in Childhood, *Clinics in Developmental Medicine*, nos 35/36. MacKeith Press.

Szasz, T. (1962) *The Myth of Mental Illness*. Secker & Warburg.

Thomas, A. and Chess, S. (1977) *Temperament and Development*. Bruner/Mazel.

West Midlands Regional Health Authority (1991) *Report of the Panel of Inquiry Appointed to Investigate the Case of Kim Kirkman*. West Midlands RHA.

World Health Organisation (1990) *International Classification of Diseases*. WHO.

Index

Added to a page number 'f' denotes a figure and 't' denotes a table.

abbreviations vii–viii
abnormality 5
acamprosate 92
acetaldehyde 92
acetylcholine 41, 84, 95
acute dystonic reactions 84, 85
acute mania 81
acute organic disorders 12–13
acute psychosis, in parents 52
adolescent psychiatry *see* child and adolescent
    psychiatry
adult mental health workers, role 59–60
advance refusal 101, 102
affective psychoses 17
    aetiology 18
    symptoms, presentation and progress 18
    treatment 19
    see also mood disorders
age, risk of infanticide 55
agoraphobia 22, 53
akathisia 84, 85
alcohol
    abuse 25, 41, 54, 91
    addiction 8–9, 26
    dependency syndrome 26
    psychotropic medication 91
    safe level 26
alienists 8
altered consciousness 24
Alzheimer's disease 13, 41, 95, 96
amisulpride 86t
amphetamines 54, 97
analgesics 73
anorexia nervosa 24, 53, 64
anti-cholinergic agents 84–5
anti-cholinesterases 95
anti-convulsants 80–1
anti-depressants 18, 73, 74–81
    adverse effects 76
    child psychiatry 66
    clinical practice points 75–6
    how they work 76
    types 74–5, 77
    use of 75
anti-epileptics 73
anti-psychotic depot injections 82
anti-psychotics 6–7

atypical 83, 86t, 87
    how they work 84
    side effects 84, 85, 87
        management of 84–5
    typical 82
    uses 83
anti-social personality disorder (ASPD) 28,
    29–30, 51
anxiety disorders 13–14, 21–3
    child and adolescent psychiatry 65
    definition 22
    in patients as parents 53
    sensation 22
anxiolytics 72
    benzodiazepines 88–9
    buspirone 90
    opiate substitution 92
    over-the-counter products 90
    sedative/hypnotic agents 89–90
    substance misuse 90–2
appearance
    in affective psychoses 18
    in mental state examinations 9
Approved Clinician 109, 110
Approved Mental Health Professionals
    legal duty 4
    liaising with nearest relatives 2
    relevant competences 3
    SOAD consultations 2–3
    use of compulsion 1
aripiprazole 86t
Asperger's syndrome 63
assessment
    child and adolescent psychiatry 61–2
    of depression 43–4
    of patients as parents 58–60
    see also mental state examinations; risk
        assessments
AMHP Guide to Mental Health Law 33, 35
asylums 8
atomoxetine (Strattera) 97, 98
attachment disorders 52, 62
attachment theory 62
attention deficit hyperactivity disorder (ADHD)
    in adults 98–9
    co-morbidity 97
    key features 97t

NICE guidelines 65
prevalence 63
stimulant medication 97–8
treatment and management 63, 64, 96–7
atypical anti-psychotics 83
comparison of 86t
drug costs 87
side effects 87
auditory hallucinations 10, 13
autism 62
automatism 35
avoidant personality disorders 27

battering 56
behaviour-oriented psychotherapy 69
behavioural and psychological symptoms of
dementia (BPSD) 96
beliefs see delusions; paranoid beliefs;
persecutory beliefs/thoughts
bendroflumethiazide 79
benzodiazepines 66, 67, 83, 88–9, 91
'best interests' principle 103
biological mechanisms, neurotic disorders 24
biological treatments 67–8
bipolar disorders 18, 80, 81
borderline personality disorder (BPD) 28, 30, 51
boys
ADHD 63
pervasive developmental disorders 62
psychiatric disorders 61
British Approved Name (BAN) 71
British National Formulary (BNF) 71
advice on prescribed drugs 55
classification headings 71–3
Code of Practice (extracts) 72
bulimia 24, 53, 64
buprenorphine 92
buproprion 91
buspirone (Buspar) 90
butyrophenones 82

capacity
and advance refusal 102
basic principles 100–1
presumption of 101
see also Mental Capacity Act
carbamazepine 80
blood level monitoring 80
practice points 80
principal uses 80
side effects 80
cardiovascular system, anti-psychotics 85

Care Quality Commission (CQC) 71, 109, 110
carers' strain, consent to treatment 105
case law 116
central nervous stimulants 73
child abuse 50, 51, 53, 55–9, 65
child and adolescent psychiatry 61–6
ADHD 63, 96–8
anxiety disorders 65
assessment 61–2
attachment 62
conduct disorder 63–4
eating disorders 64
epidemiology 61
mood disorders 65
pervasive developmental disorders 62–3
psychotic disorders 65
treatment 65–6
child homicides 50–1, 55–9
childcare, and substance abuse 54
children
of patients see patients as parents
presumption of capacity 105
Children Act 1989 59
chlordiazepoxide 91
chlorpromazine 85
cholinesterase inhibitors (CHEIs) 95
chronic alcoholism 41, 91
chronic depression 54
chronic organic states 13
chronic post-traumatic stress disorder 23
classifications
medication 71–3
psychiatry 14–15
clomethiazole 89
Clopixol Acuphase 83
cloral preparations 89
clozapine 86t, 87, 91
cocaine 54
cognitive behavioural therapy (CBT) 66
cognitive state
in affective psychoses 18
in mental state examinations 10
cognitive therapy 69
community, forensic psychiatry 32
Community Treatment Orders (CTOs) xiii, 1,
2, 108
competence, valid consent 106
compulsion, use of 1
conditionally discharged patients 37–8
conduct disorder 63–4
confidentiality 39
confusion 12, 94

consent to treatment 36t, 100 –7
  capacity *see* capacity
  child psychiatry 66
  flowchart 113
  issues 105
  mental health law 106
  sample question 115
  under Mental Capacity Act (2005) 110–13
  valid 100, 106
cot deaths 55
Court of Protection 104
criminality, and personality 48

dangerousness 38–9
decision making, test for 103
dehydration, lithium toxicity 79
deliberate self-harm 53–4, 57
delirium 94
delusions 10, 13, 18, 52
dementia 40, 94
  incidence 94
  pseudo 94
  symptoms 40, 94
  treatment and management 13, 41, 95–6
  types/sub-types 13, 41, 95f
Depakote 80
depression
  agoraphobia 22
  bipolar 18, 80, 81
  child abuse and homicide 57
  children with 65
  definition 41
  electro-convulsive therapy 68
  following from abuse 55
  maternal 51–2, 55
  monoamine theory of 18
  neurotic 23
  in old age
    aetiology 42
    assessment and treatment 43–4
    prevalence 42
    symptoms 42–3
  in parents 51–2
  in patients as parents 50
  post-natal 20, 52
  and PTSD 23
  stimulants 54
deprivation of liberty 103–4
detention
  and consent to treatment 108
  periods of 36t
dexamphetamine 97

diagnosis
  biases in 7
  mental state examinations 11
diagnostic systems 14–15
diazepam 67, 83, 91
diet, lithium toxicity 79
diminished responsibility 35
discontinuation reactions 76
disinhibited attachment disorder 62
disinhibition 40, 54
dissocial personality disorder (ASPD) 28, 29–30, 51
dissociation 24
disulfiram (Antabuse) 92
'doctrine of necessity' 103
dopamine 67, 76, 84
D'Orban study 56
drug abuse 44, 54
drug names 71
drugs
  interaction with lithium 79
  psychiatric disorders 66, 67
  side effects 67
  testing 67
  unlicensed 99
  see also individual agents
DSM 15, 27
duloxetine (SNRI) 77

eating disorders 24, 53, 64
electro-convulsive therapy (ECT) 68
environmental causes
  conduct disorder 63
  eating disorders 64
environmental risk factors, substance abuse 25
environmental therapies 70
eosinophilia myalgia syndrome (EMS) 77
ethical issues, forensic psychiatry 38–9
ethical tensions, psychiatry 7

failure to thrive 55
Falkov study 56–7
Family Law Reform Act (1969) 105
family therapy 66
fear states 51
female forensic patients 32
first episode psychosis 65, 87
flamboyant personality disorders 27
foetal alcohol syndrome 54
forensic patients 32
  care 32–3

conditionally discharged 37–8
MHRTs and discharge of 37
transfers to psychiatric hospitals 36t, 37
forensic psychiatry 32–9
definition 32–3
ethical issues 38–9
interface with the law 33–8
conditionally discharged patients under
Mental Health Act (1983) 37–8
psychiatric defences 34–5
psychiatric disposals under the Mental
Health Act (1983) 35–7
psychiatric reports 33
mental disorders and violence 33
Form T2 71, 110
Form T3 71, 110
Form T4 111
Form T5 111
Form T6 111
frontal lobe dementias 40, 95f
fugue states 24
functional disorders 12, 13

gender see boys; girls; women
genetic causes
conduct disorder 63
eating disorders 64
psychotic states 18
Geriatric Depression Scale 43
Ghosts in the nursery 55
Gillick case 66, 105, 116
girls, common psychiatric disorders 61
group therapy 69
guardianship orders 36t

hallucinations 10, 13, 18
hallucinogenics 54
haloperidol 83
Hare, Robert 30
high blood pressure 41
Hippocratic Oath 7
homicides
by mentally ill 8, 33
statistics on 48
see also child homicides; infanticide;
neonaticide
homosexuality 8
hormonal reactions, anti-psychotics 85
hospital orders 36t, 37
hybrid orders 37
hypnotics 72, 88, 89–90
hypochondriasis see somatisation disorder
hysteria 24

hysterical phenomena 23
ibuprofen 79
ICD 14–15, 27
ill health, and depression 42
infanticide 35, 55–6
infants, of depressed mothers 52, 55
information, valid consent 106
informed consent 100
Inner London Borough Study 61
inpatient work, forensic psychiatry 32
insecure attachment 52
insight
in affective psychoses 18
in mental state examinations 11
interim hospital orders 36t, 37
intersubjective approach 6
Isle of Wight study 61

justice, forensic psychiatry 32

Kim Kirkman Inquiry Panel 45
Korsakoff's disease 13, 41

L-tryptophan 77
lamotrigine 81
law
forensic psychiatry 33–8
psychiatric treatment 100–7
see also case law; mental health law
legal duties, AMHPs 4
Lewy body dementia 41, 95f
lithium carbonate 78
dosing information 78
drug interactions 79
side effects 78
toxicity 79
lorazepam 83
loss events, and depression 42

Managing Dangerous People with Severe
Personality Disorder (1999) 31
maprotiline 77
maternal anxiety 53
maternal depression 51–2, 55
maternity 'blues' 20
medical model 5–7
medication
centrality in mental illness 2
child psychiatry 66
classification 71–3
importance for AMHP 1–4
in pregnancy 54–5
prescribing information 71

see also drugs; *individual disorders*
melatonin 89
memantine (Ebixa) 96
memory requirement, decision making 102
mental capacity, and advance refusal 101
Mental Capacity Act 2005 100–5
  advance decisions to refuse treatment
      109–10
  'best interests' 103
  Court of Protection 104
  defining who lacks capacity 101
  deprivation of liberty 103–4
  key principles 100
  lasting powers of attorney 102
  memory requirement 102
  test for capacity 101
  test for making a decision 103
Mental Health Act 1983
  assessment of patients as parents 59
  capacity 108
  conditionally discharged patients 37–8
  definition of mental illness 2
  electroconvulsive therapy 68
  legal duty of the AMHP 4
  patients subject to detention under 108
  psychiatric disposals under 35–7
  psychopath (terminology) 29
  SOAD consultations 2
  Mental Health Act 2007 2, 66, 68
Mental Health Bill (2006) 2, 31
mental health law
  changes xiii
  consent to treatment 106
Mental Health Review Tribunals (MHRTs)
  access to 36t
  discharge of patients 37
Mental Health Social Work Award ix
mental illness
  debate about 8–9
  defined by Mental Health Act 2
  money, class and education 7
  psychiatric labels 2
  and violence 33
  see also neurotic disorders; psychiatric
      disorders
mental state examinations (MSEs) 9–11, 47
mentally ill, homicides by 8, 33
metabolic syndrome 85
methadone 92
methylphenidate 97, 98
mianserin 77
mirtazapine (NaSSA) 77

moclobemide 77
monoamine oxidase inhibitors (MAOIs) 74, 76t
monoamine theory of depression 18
mood
  in affective psychoses 18
  in mental state examinations 10
mood disorders 23
  borderline personality disorder 28
  child and adolescent psychiatry 65
mood stabilisers
  child psychiatry 66
  principal agents 78–81
mothers *see* maternal anxiety; maternal
      depression; patients, as parents
multi-infarction/vascular dementia 13, 95f
multiple personality disorder 24
Munchausen's syndrome by proxy 53, 57
Murray, Lynne 52

narcissistic personality disorder 30
National Health Service (NHS), psychiatrists 7
National Institute for Health and Clinical
      Excellence (NICE) 65, 81, 90, 95
National Teratology Information Service (NTIS)
      55
nausea, drugs used in 73
neonaticide 56
neuroleptics 66
neurotic disorders 13–14
  anxiety disorders 21–3, 53, 65
  co-morbidity 14
  defined 21
  demographic data 21
  mechanisms 24–5
  miscellaneous 23–4
  mood disorders 23, 65
  personality disorders 24, 26–31, 51
  substance abuse 8, 23, 25–6, 28, 90–2
nicotine addiction 8–9
nicotine replacement therapy (NRT) 91
noradrenaline 76
normal behaviour 26–7
normal personality 26–8
normalisation movement 8
normality 7
'not guilty by reason of insanity' 34

obesity, drugs used in treatment of 73
obsessive compulsive disorders 22, 53
olanzapine 83, 86t, 96
older adults 40–4
  dementia *see* dementia

depression 41–4
  other psychiatric disorders 55
  psychiatric medication 94
opiate substitution 92
opiates, problems associated with 54
OPTICS scheme 77
organic states 12–13

panic disorders 22
paranoid, defined 19
paranoid beliefs 10, 19–20
paranoid states 19
  mothers with 53
  personality disorder 19
  symptoms 19
  syndromes 19–20
paraphilias 2
paraphrenia 44
parents see patients, as parents
parkinsonism 73, 84, 85
patient risk, management 8
patients
  access to MHRTs 36t
  doctors' reluctance to think about differences
      between 7
  as parents
    assessing if child's needs are being met 50
    assessment 58–60
    child abuse and homicide 55–9
    possible risks to children 50–1
    prevalence 50
    psychiatric diagnoses and effect of these on
        parenting 51–5
    risk assessment 51, 60
  perceptions of psychiatrists 6
  subject to detention, and consent 108
  see also forensic patients
perception, assessing 10
perceptional disturbances 13
perinatal problems, with alcohol and drugs 54
persecutory beliefs/thoughts 19
person-oriented psychotherapy 69–70
personal identity states, loss of 24, 40
personality
  and criminality 48
  and eating disorders 64
  ways of thinking about 27
personality disorders 26–31
  causes 28
  child abuse and homicide 51, 57
  ICD and DSM diagnostic systems 27

key feature 27–8
  paranoid 19
  prevalence 28
  risk and 31
  risk management 48–9
  types 28–30
pervasive developmental disorders 62–3
phenothiazines 82, 85
phobic disorders 22, 53
Pick's disease 41
pimozide 85
positive attachments 19
post-natal disorders 20
  child homicides 51
  depression 20, 52
  (puerperal) psychosis 52–3
post-partum psychosis 20
post-traumatic stress disorder (PTSD) 22, 23, 25
powers of attorney 102
pregnancy, prescribed drugs in 54–5
prochlorperazine 83
professional dilemmas, assessment of parents
    59
promazine 83
propranolol 85
pseudo dementia 94
psychiatric defences 34–5
psychiatric disorders
  commonly treated 14
  drugs used in 73
  of old age 40–4
  see also mental illness; neurotic disorders;
      psychotic disorders
psychiatric disposals, under Mental Health Act
    (1983) 35–7
psychiatric labels 2
psychiatric reports 34
psychiatrists 5–11
  adoption of medical model 5–7
  role 7–9
psychiatry
  classification systems 14–15
  dualistic approach 7
  ethical tensions 7
  importance for AMHPs 1–4
  medication, classification 71–3
  organic vs. functional disorders 12–13
  psychotic vs. neurotic states 13–14
  risk assessment 45–9
  social discourses 8
  struggle for respectability 6

subjectivity 6
treatment *see* treatment(s)
see also child and adolescent psychiatry;
    forensic psychiatry
psycho-surgery 68
psychoanalysis 69
psychodynamic psychotherapy 66
psychological mechanisms, neurotic disorders
    24
psychological treatments 66, 68–70
psychopaths
    rating checklist 30
    risk management issues 48–9
    terminology 29
Psychopathy Checklist – Revised (PCL-R V2) 30
psychotherapies 66, 68–70
psychotic disorders 13
    affective psychoses 17–19
    children 65
    co-morbidity 14
    paranoid states 19–20
    patients as parents 52–3
    post-natal 20, 51, 52–3
    schizophrenia 10, 16–17, 44, 52, 65, 67
puerperal psychosis 52–3

quetiapine 86t

rapid tranquilisation programmes 83
Re C (1994) 101, 116
reactive attachment disorder 62
reboxetine (NARI) 77
recommended International Non-proprietary
    Name (rINN) 71
Reed Report (1992) 32–3
refusal of treatment, advance 101, 102
relatives, liaising with 2
remand orders 36t, 37
restriction orders 36t, 37
Retard 80
retirement, and depression 42
reversible inhibitors of monoamine oxidase
    (RIMAs) 74
risk, and personality disorder 31
risk assessments
    categories of seriousness 47
    conducting full 45–6
    key elements 46
    mental state examinations 47
    patients as parents 51, 60
risk management 8, 48–9
risperidone 86t, 87, 96

safety information, prescribed drugs 55
schizo-affective psychosis 18
schizoid personality disorders 27
schizophrenia 16
    aetiology 17
    auditory hallucinations 10
    child and adolescent psychiatry 65
    diagnosis 16–17
    in old age 44
    in parents 52
    research into, as brain disease 7
    symptoms and progress of 16
    treatment 17, 67
Schneider's first rank symptoms 16–17
school refusal 53
Scott, Peter 29
Scottish Medicines Consortium (2003) 95
Second Opinion Appointed Doctors 2, 71,
    109–12, 113t, 114–15
secure attachment 52
sedative agents 89–90
selective serotonin re-uptake inhibitors (SSRIs)
    74–5, 76t
self-esteem, of children of over-critical mothers
    52
self-harm, deliberate 53–4, 57
self-medication hypothesis 25
seriousness, categories, in risk assessment 47
serotonin (5-HT) 76
sexual deviancy 2
skin reactions, anti-psychotics 85
smoking cessation 91
social control, psychiatrists as agents of 8
social discourses, psychiatry and 8
social and environmental therapies 70
socially functional personality 27
socio-economic factors, and infanticide 56
socio-environmental causes, neurotic disorders
    24–5
sociopathy (ASPD) 28, 29–30, 51
sodium valproate 80
somatisation disorder 22, 53
speech
    in affective psychoses 18
    in mental state examinations 9
statutes 116
stimulants 54, 73, 97–8
Study of Working Together, A 56–7
subjectivity, of psychiatry 6
substance abuse 25–6
    anxiolytics 88, 90
    mental health problem debate 8

and personality disorders 28
and PTSD 23
see also alcohol abuse; drug abuse
suicide, risk 44
symptom severity, consent to treatment 105

tardive dyskinesia 84, 85
test for capacity 101
therapeutic communities 70
thiamine 91
thioridazine 85
thioxanthenes 82
thought, in mental state examinations 10
trait theory 27
trazodone 77
treatability 38
treatment(s)
   biological 67–8
   consent *see* consent to treatment
   medication *see* medication
   psychological 66, 68–70
   social or environmental 70
   see also individual disorders
tricyclic anti-depressants (TCAs) 74, 76t, 97

'unfitness to plead' 35
unlicensed drugs 99
urgent necessity, cases of 111

valid consent 68, 100, 106
valproate semi sodium 80
varenicline 91
vascular dementia 13, 95f
venlafaxine (SRNI) 77
vertigo, drugs used in 73
violence
   alcohol and depressants 54
   and mental disorders 33
   predictors of 45–6
   risk management 48–9
   to children 51
voluntariness, valid consent 107

websites, useful 117
weight gain, anti-psychotics 85
women
   forensic psychiatry 32
   neurotic disorders 21
   see also mothers

zaleplon 89–90
zolpidem 89–90
zopiclone 89–90
zotepine 86t